DYSLEXIC

My Journey

DYSLEXIC

My Journey

Michael P. Balzano, PhD

PathBinder Publishing
Virginia

Dyslexic: My Journey
Copyright © 2019 by Michael P. Balzano, PhD. All rights reserved.
Paperback ISBN: 978-0-9996048-2-3

Published by PathBinder Publishing
www.PathBinderPublishing.com

Cover Design by Gordon Torp
www.behance.net/gordontorp

Author Photo by Matthew Balzano

Dedication

To Ray Boffa

He was willing to help me as an illiterate, learning-disabled and incorrigible young man. When he offered me an opportunity to enter an optical apprenticeship, he changed my life.

To Evelyn Casey

Her vision of my potential set me on a track for college and beyond. She was an indispensable person in my life.

Contents

Contents

Foreword

This is the gripping story of how "Crazy Mikey" transformed into Dr. Michael Balzano, a much-respected member of the Washington governmental scene. It is the story of how a young man with a learning disability, but substantial innate talent, became lost in America's educational system—until one day he was found. It tells how a garbage man rose to a key position at the pinnacle of government in the White House. And, as improbable as it all seems, beyond being fascinating reading, his story offers profound lessons for us all—especially for parents, teachers and counselors of troubled youth. Sadly, it is also the story of another of the failings of many of America's 14,000 public school systems: namely, a commitment to serve mainly as a college preparatory venue.

Mike Balzano and I have long been friends, but it was not until a snowy wintry morning at a business breakfast that he shared his life's story with me. Although I had always privately marveled at his ability to be as comfortable (and impactful) in a union hall as in a Fortune 100 board room, little had I realized the importance that a few people had in his life, a life that could have gone "either way." Nor did I ever imagine that this accomplished gentleman had, throughout much of his early years, been, well, a ne'er do well. No doubt the world is full of Crazy Mikeys who have the ingrained potential to serve humanity— if only the rest of us were aware enough and took enough time to offer them a hand.

In a very minor way, my own story begins with an incident somewhat reflective of Mikey's daily fare: I was thrown out of kindergarten for bad behavior. In those days, as I was to learn, indiscretions were not to be tolerated—all much to the dismay of the loving father and mother of this only child for whom they sacrificed greatly. Years later, an influential teacher asked me what I wanted to do the following year when I graduated from the Colorado high school I was attending. Hearing my response, "I think I might like to be a forest ranger," he simply said, "No"...and handed me an envelope with an application to Princeton. He said that if I could get admitted there, they would pay my way through. I did, and they did—and another life was profoundly changed. Truly, caring people can impact young people's lives.

But there is yet another great lesson to be found between the covers of this fast-paced, provocative book. That lesson relates to the aforementioned rather singular focus of most of America's public schools on preparing all—yes, "all"—students to one day pursue a college degree. Now, I would be the last person in the world to discourage a person from pursuing a college degree if they had a reasonable chance of succeeding and, importantly, wanted to do so. But there are other choices.

In years past there was, for example, a generally available alternative path to a useful career to be found in most high schools and community colleges. That was to pursue an apprenticeship in the trades or crafts. This remains a highly respected and rewarding avenue for young people throughout Europe, particularly in Germany and England. However, in America, our community colleges have gradually drifted towards serving as preparatory schools for four-year colleges and universities—in part to offset the failings of our nation's public schools where in standardized tests of 15-year-olds the U.S. ranks 21st in science and 27th in math out of 32 developed

(OECD) nations. Math and science are of course the foundation of most jobs created in today's increasingly high-tech world.

As one learns from Crazy Mikey's early "career," our high schools and community colleges desperately need to offer an alternative learning track that leads to formal certification in a skill that is in demand. Opportunities range from computer operations to medical technician, from electrical worker to carpenter, and from aircraft maintenance to—in the case of Crazy Mikey—optical technician; all respectable, important fields that pay very competitive wages and offer the opportunity for considerable personal satisfaction—through service to others and by producing tangible outcomes to which one can point with pride.

I recall the older gentleman who built a beautiful stone fireplace for us at our home located high up in the Colorado Rockies. He worked through an entire winter in a "cocoon" he had constructed by wrapping plastic sheeting around a structure of scaffolding that contained a portable gas heater. Several months after completing the fireplace, he appeared at our front door carrying a camera and in the company of his 10-year-old grandson. He asked if we would mind taking a picture of his grandson and him standing in front of the fireplace he had built. His pride was evident, and he had good reason to be proud—just as did, for example, my own grandfather, a carpenter, who constructed beautiful inlaid work for the Pullman railroad cars of his era.

But whether one receives a college degree or a certificate in a trade, that is only the beginning. One must continue to learn throughout one's career. Many of the best jobs that will be available a decade from now have not even been invented yet, and many of the jobs that require no particular skill will be filled by robots and applications of artificial intelligence. This will relieve those with limited formal education free from boring, repetitive work—and will create new jobs for those who maintain skills. A former CEO of the Intel Corporation says that 90 percent of the revenues that the firm realizes on the last day of a fiscal year come from products that didn't even exist on the first day of that year. Similarly, it took over 70 years for the telephone to penetrate from 10 percent to 90 percent of America's homes—but the smart phone did it in just eight years. I have long thought that college diplomas and certificates in the trades should have expiration dates printed on them! The reader of this book will see why as one follows Mikey's journey pursuing new opportunities.

Fortunately, not every young person will face the learning challenges that were confronted by Mikey, but his is a life that exemplifies what can be accomplished given a suitable educational pathway...along with a few boosts from a perceptive parent, teacher, or counselor at a critical moment.

Norman R. Augustine
Retired Chairman and CEO, Lockheed Martin Corporation
Former Under Secretary of the Army
Former Professor, Princeton University School of Engineering and Applied Science

Acknowledgments

To Norm Augustine and Mike Petters, colleagues and friends of long standing, who years ago inspired and encouraged me to write this book

To Sarah Petters Fletcher whose experiences in the public schools of Georgia and Louisiana as a front-line teacher and administrator was helpful in providing me with guidance from a teacher's perspective. She reviewed several drafts of this book while working on her doctorate in education.

To Jini Leeds Clare, colleague, editor, author, and publisher, who edited articles, monographs and books I have written over the years. For this book, she was helpful because of her accomplishments in special education teaching children with physical and learning disabilities, as well as children with serious behavioral challenges.

To Rae W. Iverson, a colleague of many years, who spent years researching the laws addressing the rights of special needs children to receive appropriate education. As a public high school teacher, she worked with school counselors to place children with learning disabilities in her classes for the academic challenge and structure they needed.

To all the middle school and high school teachers and counselors, currently teaching and retired, whom I interviewed over the last several years about their work helping parents understand the options they had for educating their dyslexic children.

To Liz Prestridge and Suzanne Bentz whose insights and editing skills always make my writing better.

To Heather Hummel Gallagher who recognized the need for this book and helped organize the content and messages it contains.

To Laura Prete who urged me to describe in detail the people in the neighborhood from which this story was born.

To Chris Balzano, my son and colleague whose skillful editing of my articles, op-ed pieces, and books has been invaluable.

To my wife Denise and son Matt, both of whom encouraged and supported the writing and completion of this work.

In Memoriam

To Captain John Lee "Skip" MacMichael, US Navy retired, whose interest in apprenticeships and the need to reestablish the achievement ethic in America's young people was a guiding force for me in writing this book. Days before his passing, Captain MacMichael reviewed the last draft. I have made use of his comments and suggestions.

To Marlene Beck Anderson, colleague and protégé, who co-authored with me a study documenting the social programs of organized labor. Marlene read all the initial drafts of this book, and tirelessly pursued its completion. Sadly, we lost her a few months ago, but I see her smile in all the vignettes she selected, as it was important for her that mothers find help for their children through those stories.

To Dr. Gerald Winter, psychology professor at the University of Bridgeport who helped me obtain a Dana Scholarship at Bridgeport and urged me to apply to Georgetown University to pursue a graduate degree.

Introduction

In 2016, I published a book titled *Building a New Majority*. That book critically analyzed each presidential election between 1972 and 2012. In chapter one I revealed for the first time—to friends, corporate clients, and Washington officialdom—that I was once a learning-disabled child with dyslexia[1] that went undetected by teachers, school administrators, career counselors, and even my family.

My parents were working-class immigrants who lived paycheck-to-paycheck and qualified as the "working poor." We lived in the Italian section of New Haven, Connecticut. While other children in my neighborhood played baseball, basketball, and other team sports, I was off playing with guns and knives, wandering alone through abandoned warehouses on the waterfront, and running around among moving trains in rail yards. When I jumped off a garage roof wearing a Superman-style cape and later set a garage on fire, it was not surprising that neighborhood parents would not allow their children to play with me. My disruptive behavior took place in school and in the community. I was thrown out of one Catholic school, one public school, and later the military. Neighbors called me "Crazy Mikey," a term that stuck with me through my mid-twenties.

I dropped out of high school at 16 and wandered through dozens of minimum wage jobs, from which I was fired, quit, or simply chose not to show up for work. Not surprisingly, it became impossible for me to obtain employment in my hometown. With the help of a Democratic ward leader, my family arranged for me to work for New Haven's Department of

Sanitation as a garbage collector. I held down this job until a back injury made lifting heavy objects impossible. My career as a garbage man was over.

Despite my antisocial and unsuccessful beginning, I went on to enter an optical apprenticeship, became a licensed optician, and managed an optical company. I eventually left that career to enter the University of Bridgeport as a history major where I graduated *magna cum laude*. I was awarded a fellowship to Georgetown where I received a PhD with distinction in Political Theory.

My life story, and working-class history was featured on the front page of a Washington, DC newspaper; the headline read, "Garbage Man to PhD."[2] The article was read by Jerry Jones, Director of Personnel at the Nixon White House, and appeared at the very time President Nixon was looking for someone who could communicate with working-class Americans living in inner-city ethnic neighborhoods in the Northeast and Midwest states. Because they read the article, I became the third-highest ranking Democrat in the Nixon White House and the person the national press called, "the President's Ambassador to Middle America." I was later appointed by the President to direct a federal agency that included all federally funded volunteer programs, including the Peace Corps. I went on to advise six U.S. Presidents, four Secretaries of Defense, multiple generals and admirals.

In a span of 12 years, I went from a learning-disabled class failure to top scholar in two universities; from one unable to hold a job to eventually advising CEOs of America's largest corporations on workforce issues.

On the lecture circuit, scores of parents, teachers, and guidance counselors have asked me the following questions seeking to prepare "challenged" students to be productive citizens. They all wanted to know: What turned me around? How did I overcome my antisocial behavior? How did I go from class failure to top scholar?

Upon learning of my history, two of my corporate clients—Norm Augustine, former CEO of Lockheed Martin, and Mike Petters, the CEO of Huntington Ingalls Industries—both of whom I regard as stewards of society, urged me to write a book to answer those questions and to describe the challenges I faced in overcoming my learning disabilities and antisocial behavior. They reasoned that it was important for current and future high school dropouts with learning disabilities and behavior issues similar to mine to use my experience as a "roadmap" for overcoming their own disabilities. Having been asked so many times to comment on overcoming my learning disabilities, I have written this overview of my life and work history in the hope that it might be useful to parents and educators dealing with children with learning disabilities.

Several audiences will find this book useful. First, parents of children engaged in antisocial behavior that may be caused by undetected learning disabilities. Second, grade school and middle school teachers dealing with problem students. Third, school counselors who are advocating career paths for students upon completing high school or before dropping out.

This book is both an autobiography and an action plan to help young people with learning disabilities cope with those disabilities in a positive way. I inform parents with children of grammar school age to be alert to behavior problems of their children that could mask undetected learning disabilities. I also advise such parents to be persistent with school officials and to seek the help they need for their children.

The book attempts to help teachers in both elementary and middle school to identify children with special needs who have been allowed to pass from one grade to another without identifying or addressing particular learning disabilities.

The middle section of this book addresses the critical role of school counselors. For the last 30 or more years, school systems have focused on encouraging students to attend college while all but ignoring other options. Going to college has become a priority not just for the schools but for the parents who want to provide their children with an education that will yield a better life. But this focus on a college degree as the key to a better life has excluded other avenues to obtain that same goal. Here I focus on the advantages for students to explore a career that involves an apprenticeship to a master craftsman in any of the crafts associated with the industrial arts.

For most of the 20th century, the industrial arts constituted a conveyor belt on which millions of Americans rode into the middle class. Having been abandoned in the 1970s, that conveyor belt is now being recreated with the rebirth of America's manufacturing sector and new jobs. These are not the old, dirty manufacturing jobs of the 20th century. These require a level of training and education associated with modern manufacturing. These are higher paying jobs that produce incomes every bit as high as one would obtain after borrowing thousands of dollars to obtain a college degree in subjects for which there are no jobs. Here is where the role of school counselor is vital.

Finally, the last part of this book is a testimonial to the teachers who taught in the inner-city public schools in the 1940s and 50s. My learning disabilities made it impossible for me to demonstrate to them that they had taught me anything. But in fact, they gave me a different kind of confidence. I could not have made it without the confidence my teachers gave me about myself and my country.

PART I
My Story

Chapter 1

Crazy Mikey

My third-grade classroom was noticeably empty. Only a few pupils were told to remain seated when the rest of the class was promoted to the next room where they would begin the fourth grade. I had been through this drill before at St. Michael's, a Catholic school a few blocks away from the public school I was now attending. At St. Michael's, on promotion day, all the children wore white. With pride in their accomplishments, they were ceremoniously marched into an adjacent room by the nun who had been their teacher throughout the year. In the next room another nun eagerly awaited her new students. Those who were required to repeat the year sat silent and somber as the class was promoted. In the public school it was the same; for most students, not being promoted was not a happy occasion.

That year, there was a young boy brought in from another class and told that he would have to repeat the year. His name was Tommy Scelzo. He cried loudly with tears flowing down his red face. I tried to comfort him by saying that everything was going to be fine—there would be a new bunch of kids coming in to start third grade; we would make new friends, and we could laugh and clown around together. Tommy and I became friends for the rest of our lives until he died in his late 70s just a few years ago.

As I reflect on that school day, it is clear to me that Tommy took having to repeat third grade as shameful while I was perfectly comfortable failing in the public school as I had failed in the Catholic school.

Failure was just normal to me. There was no shame or feeling that I was inferior to the other students. Nor would I ever cry about it. I felt neither shame nor embarrassment. For me, even at that age, failure was a fact of life.

WOOSTER SQUARE

I grew up in an Italian section of New Haven, Connecticut, known as Wooster Square. Like other industrial centers in the Northeast, New Haven was populated by European immigrants who worked in the numerous factories and machine shops that made New England a magnet for this new generation of twentieth century pilgrims. Whether they were Italians, Germans, Poles, Greeks, or Lithuanians, they all found employment in that rapidly growing part of the country. Although the points of origin of those who flocked to America varied, most who came shared a number of common characteristics. Some were entrepreneurs who came in search of business opportunities. Others were skilled tradesmen who were in short supply in America. The majority, however, were unskilled workers who left their native countries with less than a grade school education. Many of this last group were European subsistence farmers or common laborers who came to America in search of opportunities not to be found in their feudal societies. Regardless of their level of skills or the language they spoke, they came to America ready and willing to work—and to work hard.

This generation of new Americans grouped together in little neighborhoods which took on the appearance of their native European communities. In many ways, the neighborhood in which I lived was a city unto itself. It was quite possible to meet all of the needs of the people who lived in the neighborhood without ever leaving the confines of a square mile. Indeed, many of the people in that neighborhood—save for the journey to the New World—worked, prayed, played, brought up families, grew old, and died, never having left the Italian speaking part of the city known as the Wooster Square area. Wooster Street was the main artery of the neighborhood, running some ten blocks in length. The street was dotted with small family-owned businesses of all varieties. The storefront windows of these little shops served as a first-floor pedestal upon which stood the remaining portions of the three- and four-story brick apartment buildings.

At almost any hour of the day or night in a three-block section of Wooster Street, one could capture the essence of that community whose sounds and smells announced the time of day more beautifully than the chimes of any timepiece. The dawn was filled with the scent of freshly baked bread. The baker, who also delivered the bread to the local stores, filled the air with song. As he walked along the twilight-illuminated street pulling his small wagon filled with bread, the little silver-haired man in his gleaming white pants, T-shirt, and flour-covered shoes stood out against a background of the asphalt streets and dark red brick buildings which lined them. To see and hear him was to understand that Mr. Midolo approached his singing with the same intensity with which he baked his bread. He sang as though the street and buildings were the stage props of an opera. At the top of his voice he sang to people he met scurrying to work in the murky light. As he pulled his wagon, he would pause to punctuate the high and low tones with his free hand. I remember the many times when my mother was delivering me to my grandmother, who served as the day-care center for some of her working married children. We would meet Mr. Midolo, who would stop and sing to us as we passed by. When there were no people on the street, early risers would watch from their second- and third-floor windows as he sang to the half-sleeping dogs and cats that crouched in the doorways below. When the streets were void of both man and beast, Mr. Midolo would pause and, as if he were playing to an audience, raise his arm, arch his head and shoulders back and sing to the buildings themselves. This urban rooster and his songs, coming as they did with the morning sun, signaled the new day.

As the day progressed from early to mid-morning, you could hear the rubbing of squeegees against windows and bristled brooms pushing water over the newly hosed-down sidewalks as the little stores opened for business. As the sun climbed the sky, the sounds and smells changed with the passing hours. I remember the many times during the hot summer days when my grandmother would walk my cousin Marie Travisano and me along the street for her mid-afternoon social. As we passed the various storefronts, the multicolored canopies which shaded the windows and display stands before them resembled a continuous parade of flags. I was old enough to talk and understand the Italian conversations between my grandmother and passersby, but not old enough to be conscious of my age. But everything else I remember vividly. I remember the days we walked Wooster Street, which to me was one continuous mixture of odors, colors and sounds.

There was the fish market with its street-side tubs of codfish (*bacala*) being rinsed in continuously running water. Displayed in the window sat large glass aquariums with lobster, squid, and even live octopus. A few feet away was a little store that sold coffee and many kinds of freshly roasted nuts. Everywhere the smell of roasting coffee beans filled the air. A few steps up the street in either direction were two pastry shops from which the sweet fragrance of pastry shells, chocolate and vanilla cream, and rum-flavored yellow cake gave the air an almost perfume scent. Here, Grandma always bought us a lemon ice.

Still further down the street, the smell of shoe polish and rubber-based glue, along with the blunted thud-like pounding of the cobbler's hammer, announced that the shoemaker was at work. Moving right along, we passed the barber shop, with its odor of hair tonic and witch hazel. Right beyond it was a little candy store whose proprietor, between customers, sat on a chair at the rear of the store playing a guitar. Then there was the Italian Men's Club—and when I say Italian, I mean Italian! The whiff of Italian cigars, both stale and fresh, mixed with beer and traces of wine, was present. As long as I can remember, whenever we passed the Men's Club or went into the Club to ask my grandfather for a nickel, we could hear men arguing violently, some even shouting at each other at the top of their voices. As I grew older, I learned that they were not angry; they merely talked to each other in that tone of voice all the time.

I remember passing the chicken market whose sights and sounds were fascinating to a child. The clucking and cackling of the live chickens, which craned their necks through the wooden bars of the coops, were enough to hypnotize me. I often reached into the cage grabbing chickens by the neck only to be yelled at and dragged away. Often my grandmother would stop at St. Michael's Catholic Church. Built in the 1870s by an Italian order of priests, the church was reminiscent of Italian architecture with three main entrances and stained-glass windows that ran from the entrances to the back of the building. Over the door was a statue of St. Michael holding a sword in his hand and donning a bright metal breastplate vanquishing Lucifer. My grandmother told me that I was named after St. Michael. The dome of the church appeared as bright blue turquoise, which was a perfect color atop the white building. Decades later in a restoration of the church, we found that the dome was actually copper that looked like gold. To me the blue turquoise always seemed more fitting. In any case, as of this day, the dome has oxidized and is now blue turquoise once again. There were three main Protestant churches that stood on what was called the New Haven Green, a large, wrought-iron fenced park near Yale University. These churches dated from the period before the American Revolution. While there were other Catholic churches that were attended by Poles, Slavs, and French residents, St. Michael's was the central gathering point for Italians and was the largest Italian church in the state.

Late afternoon and into the night, the smells and sounds changed once again. The numerous pizza places emitted the smells emanating from giant brick ovens brought from Italy. It was difficult to distinguish the odors—the sausage from the onions, the mushrooms from the bacon, the mozzarella from the tomatoes, or the dough itself. Nor was it possible to distinguish from which place of business the odors came; they all seemed to float together on the night air. With this, too, was the smell of vinegar, spices, and fresh clams, all of which mingled with the chill odor of ice.

Wooster Street is nationally famous for its pizzerias, established in the early 1900s when the Italians arrived in America. Each pizzeria offered a somewhat different style of pizza reminiscent of the different places in Italy from which the owners emigrated. The pizzas were baked in coal-fired brick ovens brought from Italy. Your hands would be left with a residue of coal dust that was inevitably baked into the bottom of the pizza. No one worried about carcinogens.

The first pizzeria encountered on Wooster Street was Sally's, which was opened in 1938. The pizza here was very thin and had to be eaten with a knife and fork, not folded over as people normally eat pizza today. Sally's claim to fame was that occasionally Frank Sinatra ate there. There were photos on the kitchen wall and newspaper articles to testify about the Sinatra visits. Directly across the street was a more formal restaurant called Rossetti's. Here the waiters wore tuxedos and bow ties.

One block down Wooster Street was a quaint pizzeria named Sarno's, which was also a restaurant. Sarno's definitely was not as formal as Rossetti's, but with a grape arbor in the backyard, Sarno's boasted an Italian atmosphere.

Directly across the street from Sarno's was The Spot, my family's favorite pizzeria along with all of my boyhood friends. Ernie Boccomiello, who ran The Spot in the early days, also operated a chicken market in the building next door. You could not tell if the red stain on his white apron was tomato sauce or chicken blood. He used to run back and forth between the two buildings until the health department forced him to choose between the two businesses. Fortunately, he chose the pizzeria. The Spot appeared in a book titled *The Best in America,* which claimed to identify things like the best steak house, the best hamburgers, and so on. When it identified the best pizza in America they listed "The Spot on Wooster Street."

Then there was Pepe's Pizzeria, opened in 1925. Unlike the other pizzerias, Pepe's was the most commercial. To this day, it still has a large sign with a man in a white hat holding a pizza. Pepe's is the pizzeria that is frequented less by the locals and caters mostly to Yale students.

Finally, there was Cocco's—not on the main drag of Wooster Street but a few blocks away on St. John Street. Cocco used the same style of brick oven but cooked the pizza in a metal tin so that there was no coal dust on the pizza crust like all the other pizzerias. (On a side note, I dated and later married Cocco's granddaughter, Emily, whom I met in the neighborhood as a teenager.)

Wooster Street was so famous for its Italian history that during the presidential campaign of 1980, I took Ronald Reagan to Wooster Street to speak before the Society of St Mary Magdalene, the oldest Italian society in the state. During his visit, Reagan had a slice of pizza at Pepe's, which was the only pizzeria open in the afternoon. We then went to Libby's Italian Pastry Shop to try the lemon ice of my childhood. When the campaign plane left that evening, Ralph Marcarelli, who spoke at Reagan's event, delivered a large tray of Libby's famous cookies for everyone on the plane who were not able to make the stops along Wooster Street with Reagan.

It was a safe community in which to live—safe from anyone who could come into a neighborhood and do harm to the residents. The neighbors knew each other and would politely challenge anyone who didn't belong there. "Hi. Are you looking for someone?" Or, "You seem to be looking for someone. Can I help you?" No one in our community ever had their homes robbed by outsiders nor would any member of the community do harm to another member. In that first generation of immigrants from southern Italy there was a tendency to deal severely with anyone who hurt others in the neighborhood. We did not call the police. Unquestionably, the neighborhood was safe and secure. Wooster Street was not a Hobbesian state of nature, but any neighbor breaking the rules would be severely punished and there was no appeal. Law and justice were important to Italians in our community because from the earliest days of their arrival to the United States they were beset upon by a criminal element that came from Sicily called the "Black Hand." This sense of community justice was something totally acceptable to the residents of our neighborhood because it created a peaceful environment in which immigrant parents could bring up their children. And it was peaceful. The children were free to play in the neighborhoods.

I remember the days when my cousin Marie, who was only eight months older than I, took charge of me when, without my grandmother, we sat barefooted on a giant brown granite curbstone as the steel-rimmed wheels on horse-drawn wagons of Smedley's Freight Moving Company passed within inches of our toes as they returned the Clydesdale-like horses back to the stalls a block from my grandmother's apartment. I also remember the chain-driven Mac Bulldog trucks that rumbled through the streets of our neighborhood. We were nine years old in that hot summer of 1944. All of our male cousins were either in the Army, the Navy, or the Marine and were in

Australia, France, or on the Island of Saipan. I can feel the heat of that day and the smell of those horses as I write these words.

THE SMELL OF AN
INDUSTRIAL COMMUNITY

But there were other sounds and smells in the streets that called to mind different scenes—ones that conjured up visions of hard-working people. The loud hoot of the seven o'clock whistle on the roof of Sargent Hardware Company signaled for the residents of our neighborhood and the hundreds of Polish, Lithuanian, and other ethnic neighborhoods in the surrounding area, the beginning of another workday. I recall the summer when I was just old enough to explore the cross streets that served to measure the blocks of Wooster Street. The area was filled with large and small machine shops that made and repaired all kinds of machine tools. As you walked along the various wide streets, once again the sounds and smells told you about the community. On one block the unsynchronized whirring sounds of sewing machines came through the open windows of the Brewster Shirt Company. On another there was the acrid smell of welding flux and the high-pitched blowing sounds of acetylene torches whose flashes, as well as shower of sparks, told you that metal was being welded. Along the Water Street area were the large manufacturing companies, which produced a wide variety of hard goods.

My mother was born in America, of working-class Italian immigrants who came to America in the late 1800s, while two of her five siblings were born in Italy. My father and four of his siblings arrived from

Italy in 1906. Both families settled in an area of New Haven, Connecticut.

My family today would be described as the working poor. My parents lived from paycheck to paycheck in a three-room cold-water flat. There were two bedrooms—one that I shared with my older brother and one where my parents slept. There was no central heating system. Only the kitchen was heated with an oil stove, and as with most families it was the central meeting place in the apartment. For a short time, my father had an unvented oil burner in my bedroom, which our doctor said would kill us if we didn't keep the windows open. This, of course, defeated the reason for the oil burner!

In the kitchen was a metal-topped table and six unmatched wooden straight-back chairs with no padding on the seats. I still have two of those chairs that I kept in memory of our home. In addition to having no heat or hot water, no telephone or television, we had only a toilet and no bathing facility. To bathe, we heated water in a tea kettle and took sponge baths. I couldn't wait to be old enough to go to the YMCA to take a real shower. The apartment was extremely cold in the winter; you could see your breath in either of the bedrooms. My older brother and I pretended we were dragons breathing the chilled vapors at each other.

We did not own a refrigerator. We were the only people I knew of who still had an icebox in the 1940s. Aside from being very small and unable to keep food from spoiling, which happened constantly, we had an iceman who delivered a large block of ice weekly. As I think of it now, my mother was extremely embarrassed when he arrived. It was even more embarrassing when, in winter, my father would use man-sized icicles that fell from our roof instead of calling the iceman. It was hard to explain to our neighbors why we were taking fallen icicles into our apartment. We had no car; my parents always walked to work or took public transportation, which throughout my childhood was trolley cars that were open in the summer and closed tight in the winter.

At dinner my parents would talk about their day's experience. Unlike his parents, who were farmers in Italy and had settled in a farming community in rural North Haven, my father moved into the industrial center of the city of New Haven. He worked in one of the dozens of large factories in the area. He became a milling machine operator at Winchester Repeating Arms Company, one of the oldest gun makers in America. In time, he became a highly skilled machinist whose work was held to within a thousandth of an inch. My father was a proud member of the International Association of Machinists, which he credited with providing him with his wages and benefits. During World War II, he worked six days a week, ten hours a day. He was intellectually inquisitive. He went from speaking Italian in his childhood to speaking perfect English in his teens. He constantly looked up words in the dictionary to determine their precise meaning. At one point, he bought a slide rule and confessed his frustration that he couldn't figure out how it worked. It is clear to me that had he been given any training at all, he would surely have advanced his position in the company where he worked.

My mother worked at Sargent Lock and Hardware Company, the nation's oldest manufacturer of door and window locks. During her career at Sargent, on two separate occasions the power press that she worked on amputated the tips of her fingers. She was transferred to a foot press where she would kick a lever that forced a piece of brass to be bent and then moved on to the next operation.

In 1941, New England factories, large and small, converted their operations to defense-related products. My mother made brass links that held bullets together in machine gun belts and bomb shackles that released bombs under the wings of fighter aircraft. In the red brick factory buildings in which they worked, there was no air conditioning. Sometimes at dinner my parents would talk about people passing out in temperatures that exceeded 100 degrees. In later life, I entered those abandoned buildings and remarked to myself that they were right out of a Dickens novel. My mother's company had no union and few benefits. There was a pension plan offered for years of service worked. However, this was not available to her because of a break in her service following my birth. My mother worked almost to delivery time when she was sent home for fear that a baby would be born on the shop floor. I was born in the home of a neighbor two days later. When my mother returned to work, she was told that her previously accrued years of service would not count toward retirement. When Sargent was later unionized, the union contract did not cover her lost years of service.

I remember many nights when my father would remove brass slivers from my mother's skin where the blower that blew slivers from the kick press would strike her exposed chest, arms and fingers. Sometimes the removal hurt because they were so deeply embedded in the skin. Removing the brass slivers required tweezers. In my father's case, steel slivers were more easily removed from his chest because in addition to the tweezers, my mother was able to use a magnet to help pull the sliver from the skin.

When I was old enough, my parents enrolled me in St. Michael's preschool and kindergarten where discipline was the order of the day. Sister Pierre exercised control over the six grades taught at St. Michael's, but also oversaw the kindergarten classes where she assessed the caliber of students entering the grade school. Kindergarten to me was a social event. Children sat in circles, ate crackers, sang songs, and were told by the nuns about Jesus and his love for us. Periodically, the parish priest visited our sessions, as did Mother Superior. Often some of the nuns who taught in the school would also visit the kindergarten class. One thing that was clear was the hierarchy that existed within the school. The parish priest was in charge, followed by Mother Superior, and then Sister Pierre. Kindergarten set a tone of order and discipline. From my earliest days it was clear I had neither.

LEARNING DISABILITIES
AND BEHAVIOR PROBLEMS

In terms of actual learning, lessons began with the alphabet printed on black and white cards that stretched above the green slate board. The teachers, all nuns, pronounced each letter, and the students repeated their words. I had no problem repeating the sing-song pattern we said in unison. But, from the earliest days, when I looked at the printed alphabet cards, periodically the letters appeared to me in reverse order. I remember singing the letters ABC but seeing C and B reversed. The same was true of N and M or T and S. I remember it because it became easier for me to rely on the sing-song pattern to recite the alphabet than it was to read the letters in sequence by looking at them.

The same thing occurred with numbers. Adjacent to the board showing the alphabet cards was another board where Arabic numerals were depicted from one to ten. As with the sing-song pattern of the alphabet, we were encouraged to say the numbers out loud. Like the experience with the alphabet, periodically, the numbers I saw were in a different order than what was on the chalkboard.

In the first grade, we began to write short words using the alphabet; for example, CAN, GOOD, BAD, etc. Almost immediately, I had a problem spelling because the letters in these words would shift. For example, for the word "CAN," I would see "CNA." With numbers, I had the same problem. I could not add or subtract because I would see different numbers on the flash cards presented to the class. I remember being promoted to the second grade where my visual problem made reading out loud almost impossible. Instead of simply reading the words, I would have to study each word before I said it out loud. The other kids did not have this problem. It was about this time when kids in the class began to snicker openly when I read. I became so self-conscious of their snickers that I just stopped reading out loud and the nun moved on to the next child. My mother was called to the school where she was told that I would have to repeat second grade.

Had teachers been trained to identify learning-disabled students at the time I was in elementary school, it would have been clear that I was dyslexic. In my case, dyslexia means letters appear to shift in words and sentences. The same is true for numbers. My dyslexia was not diagnosed until much later, when I was in my late 40s. It is ever-present when I read or add numbers. Today, eight out of ten phone numbers that I dial will turn out to be a wrong number.

Unable to participate in class lessons, I became the class clown. I threw paper airplanes and spit balls across the room and squirted kids with a water pistol I hid in my lunch box. For such actions, I was made to sit in front of the room on a stool wearing a dunce cap, facing the wall next to the nun's desk.

In first grade, when my mother was late picking me up after school, I was sent to the convent, where I was told the non-teaching nuns would punish me. But I was never punished. The nuns, who were either Italian girls in their late teens, or women in their late sixties, loved this little six-year-old boy who looked like the child they dreamed of having. They fed me pasta, minestrone, and freshly baked cookies. When my mother finally arrived, she was told that I was a wonderful little boy and that she could leave me with them anytime. I was not punished, and my mother went home none the wiser.

The nuns who taught in the school were demanding. I had to repeat the first grade, and on the condition that if I did not improve, I would be asked to leave. I did not improve, and my mother was told that she should enroll me in a public school, where standards were lower. In both first and second grades, the nuns failed to identify my learning disability.

From kindergarten on, I was a problem. I disrupted other students—laughing, joking, and fighting with other boys. I was spanked constantly. When spanking did not help, I was forced to sit quietly in the front of the room, wearing a girl's dress, and a bow clipped to my hair. This did not have the desired effect of embarrassing me. While it made other kids fearful of Catholic discipline, it didn't frighten me at all. I enjoyed making the other kids laugh. Ironically, it was in pre-school that I was enlisted by the nuns to help keep the other kids in order by telling them stories. From time to time, the nuns saw me talking to small groups of preschoolers, who sat quietly while I repeated one of the episodes of "Superman" or "The Lone Ranger" I had listened to on the radio that week. I remember being summoned by Sister Pierre. I thought she was going to spank me for something, but was surprised to learn she wanted me to help keep the children quiet by telling them one of my stories.

While my dyslexia interfered with my reading, spelling, and solving basic arithmetic problems, it did not affect my ability to pronounce words or recite conversations that I overheard. If I heard it, I could repeat it. During the war years, and all through the 1940s, the airways were filled with evening radio broadcasts of adventure programs that young children, especially boys, listened to nightly. During those years, I was glued to the radio in our kitchen between 5:00 and 8:00 pm. "The Lone Ranger," "Tom Mix," "Superman," "Jack Armstrong All American Boy," "Green Hornet," "Terry and the Pirates," "Sky King," and more—I never missed a program. In fact, I began memorizing the stories as I listened to them, which increased my vocabulary tremendously.

Today I realize that in my early years I learned English not from the public school system but from the radio programs that were part of my daily routine. My vocabulary, pronunciation and usage came from all of the different radio broadcasts and the movies my mother would take me to see. I remember overhearing some of my teachers actually saying to each other that they could not understand why my vocabulary was so clearly superior to all the other students in the class, and yet I could not read or write the same words I spoke. The ability to memorize words and dialogue became a lifelong advantage for me. Whenever information was spoken to me, I simply recorded that message in my mind. Later, I was able to repeat that story or lecture whenever requested.

When I entered the public school, I was already so far behind the other students that my parents were advised to move me to another less demanding public school. I was enrolled in the Dante School, a public school a few blocks from our home. As a mid-year transfer student, I never caught up with the other students, so repeating third grade was inevitable. But given what I have already said, one can see why staying back, i.e., failing third grade, did not upset me in the least.

Unfortunately, having an excellent memory did not help me survive in school. Because I did not participate in normal schoolwork like the other children, I became a constant nuisance. I laughed and joked with other disorderly students and was singled out as a malcontent and the instigator of trouble. When I entered my second public school, the teachers were already on notice about my poor academic performance and my antisocial behavior. In my first public school, my mother had been summoned to meet with my teachers in hopes that my family could straighten me out. With less than a sixth-grade education, my parents could do little to help me with my homework. In addition, once World War II began, both of my parents spent endless hours in the factory.

Helping their child with homework assignments was not possible.

The antisocial behavior was another story. My mother had been called out of work so many times that she was now in danger of losing her job. She simply could not attend school meetings during the daytime. That was when my Aunt Mary (Perrelli) became my surrogate mother. She worked in a gift shop and had flexible hours. She also lived in an apartment beside St. Michael's School, and a half block from Columbus School, the third public school I attended. She was the one who was originally told by the nuns at St. Michael's that although they loved me, I was unable to perform at the level they required and that I should be sent to public school. Here again, though the nuns were excellent teachers, they did not detect my dyslexia. It was my Aunt Mary who helped to get me settled into public school.

In Columbus School, it was clear that the name Balzano raised concerns among the teachers and administrators. On my very first day at school, I was notified by my homeroom teacher that my presence in her room gave her cause for concern, not because of my reputation, but because of her experience with my older brother. As Mrs. Connor called the roll of new students on that first day, she paused when I answered yes to Balzano. She stopped after I responded and read my full name again. When I again responded Balzano, she motioned for me to come to her desk.

She was a very large woman who demonstrated her strength by grabbing my necktie and pulling my head down beside hers and asked if I had a brother named Anthony Balzano. When I answered yes, she pulled me around in front of her so that my face was inches away from her eyeglasses. I could smell the strong perfume she wore and the smell of coffee on her breath. "I want you to be a good boy, do you understand me—a good boy," she said. She continued in a serious voice, "I never want your father to be called to school because of your behavior. Do you hear me?" she said, twisting my tie tighter around her fist, pulling me closer. "You need to talk to Mr. O'Hara, the school principal, right now."

"But I didn't do anything," I protested.

"I want you to go to the principal's office and tell him I sent you down to meet with him," she replied.

Mr. O'Hara was busy with first day of school issues and was initially confused by my appearance in his office. When I told him my name, he suddenly became very calm. "Michael Balzano," he repeated my name and then asked, "Do you have a brother named Anthony?" He removed his eyeglasses and told me to sit down. He repeated Mrs. Connor's admonition that it was important for me to be a good boy. "We do not want to send for your father if you misbehave. We would like to resolve any problems ourselves. So, if there are any problems with your teachers, I want you to bring them here in my office. My door will always be open to you." He asked me about my personal interests, and I told him of my interest in World War II fighter planes. To my delight, he produced a magazine that contained an entire section of World War II fighters and bombers. He pointed to a desk in his outer office and told me he would give me tracing paper to trace the airplanes in the magazine. He then repeated Mrs. Connor's words concerning not having my father called to school.

I questioned my Aunt Mary about all this, and she told me that my father had been called to the school because my brother had thrown a knife at the desk of another student. My father lost his cool and began to punch and kick my brother right in front of the class. Mrs. Connor was terrified and started screaming. Other teachers responded to her screams and pounced upon my father, pulling my brother free. Mr. Harter, then principal of the school, came running to the room and was also involved in extracting my father from the room. It was a horrifying experience for everyone. More importantly, since I was already identified as a troublemaker, the possibility of any parental visit to discipline me was terrifying to many of the same teachers who witnessed the earlier event.

From my first day at public school, it was my Aunt Mary who met with my teachers when I ran afoul of the rules, which was often. I was constantly in the principal's office tracing pictures of airplanes and warships. When I realized that neither my teachers nor Mr. O'Hara were concerned about my whereabouts and were not monitoring me, I left his office and wandered through the waterfront or rail yard a few blocks from the school.

When I did attend class, I appeared totally unresponsive to the teacher's lectures. I say "appeared" because even though I looked like a corpse in class, I was listening to Miss Horowitz as she described the ancient civilizations her class covered. Like the radio programs I listened to each night, I mentally recorded her talks. I did the same thing with the poems read by Miss Lowenbaum, my English teacher, who read Shakespeare's Macbeth. aloud to the class. When tests were given, I could not read the questions or answer them, so I constantly failed. But I was promoted each year to get me out of the class. I continued to be the class clown, laughing, joking and interrupting the other students.

Unlike the other kids, I did not like sports of any kind. I sat on the bench refusing to participate. Once in middle school, the physical education department chartered a bus to New York to attend a baseball game at Yankee Stadium. Six of the more troubled students conspired to abandon the group once we arrived at the ballpark and went instead to Times Square. We all looked older than we were. We bought wine and took a classic photo in one of the street arcades. The faculty guidance counselors who were on the trip were frantic when they could not find us at the stadium. There were no more field trips for that class after that. Although I was not the ringleader of that group, I was blamed for having coaxed the others to leave the ballpark. In fact, I had wanted to see the game. I had never been to a ballgame. I was in my mid-seventies when a client took me to see the Washington Nationals and explained the role of each of the players.

All this antisocial behavior took a serious turn when Aunt Mary was called by school officials who warned that my antisocial behavior was caused by deep psychological problems and should be addressed. With my Aunt Mary's approval, I attended a series of sessions with psychologists retained by the school to make assessments about my mental stability. I remember the meetings with both men and women psychologists who administered a battery of tests which focused on spatial relationships, color charts, and stacking small wooden blocks. My aunt was told the tests did not point to anything that could stop my antisocial behavior. They concluded that my behavior required an examination by a psychiatrist.

At thirteen, I met with a noted New Haven psychiatrist named Dr. Rotamacher. He was a soft-spoken man who wore a bow tie. We sat in large, padded easy chairs across from each other. He did not focus on tests or diagrams but asked about my interests. I told him I was interested in rocket ships and space travel. As we talked, I could tell he was impressed with my knowledge of Greek, Roman, and Egyptian history and was intrigued by my knowledge of newly released information on the mechanics of nuclear sciences I had learned from the radio programs I monitored. The atomic bomb had just ended World War II and my radio programs talked about nuclear physics. He asked questions about my interest in history, especially how I remembered the class discussions about the Greeks and Roman battles and noted that I had never written any of this information in a notebook. He would stop from time to time to write what I said in a notebook. He asked why I did not play team sports with other children. I told him that I just didn't care for sports; I would much rather draw pictures of airplanes and ships. Asked what kind of ship, I responded that I liked to draw all kinds. He asked me to draw a ship for him, and I quickly drew a three-masted schooner in full sail with all the riggings. He kept the drawing and closed the book.

My father attended our final session. The doctor told my father that, if I had any deep psychological problems, he could not detect them. He also said there are many people who are not sports enthusiasts; he included himself in that group. He concluded that my disinterest in classroom lectures had no impact on my ability to process and store vast quantities of information. He said that I had enormous potential and ought to be enrolled in a private school that was better suited to develop my talents, especially exploiting my ability to memorize lectures. The suggestion of a private school was far beyond the ability of my parents to consider.

The truth is that I would not have wanted to attend a private school. It would have destroyed the fantasy world in which I lived. I was an urban Tom Sawyer who wandered in dangerous environments and loved adventure. Down the end of most of the cross streets and within two blocks of my house was the waterfront. New Haven was a major port on the Long Island Sound. The docks were always busy with coal and oil tankers unloading their cargoes. After 6:00 p.m., when the workers would leave the yards, the neighborhood kids had their chance to jump into the mountainous piles of coal. Whether we pretended that the avalanching pieces of coal were shifting desert sands or crumbling icebergs, the scene was enough to mentally transport imaginative kids to faraway places—images shattered only by the shouts of the watchman who came running to throw us out. I played on coal barges and watched giant oil tankers unloading cargo. I wandered through rail yards where passenger and freight lines moved on tracks in front and behind me. I remember the look on the faces of train engineers when they saw this twelve-year-old kid standing on the tracks as they passed.

LOOKING THROUGH THE WINDOWS

Along the Water Street area were large manufacturing companies, which produced a wide variety of hard goods. On any side street in my neighborhood one could get a vivid picture of industrial New England. On every block the sounds were similar and yet different. From just about every building came the sound of pounding drop forges, the high-pitched chatter of milling machines, the squeal of drill presses, and the screaming of grindstones. Behind the different sounds of these instruments of production was the ever-present hum of giant electric motors and the rumbling sound of belt-driven pulleys. The air on these streets was filled with the odors of atomized oil, burning grease, and rubber insulation from miles of overheated wiring.

All during those summers in which I was old enough to wander alone, I worked my way through the different side streets looking into the basement and ground floor windows at the various machines being operated. Through one window I used to watch the rows of drill press operators who stood before their machines pressing down the arm that lowered the drill through the metal. I liked to watch the curling strips of hot brass, copper, and steel which rose smoking around the spinning drill. My father operated a drill press for a good part of the time he spent at Winchester. While he described that particular job as cleaner than most others he had had, he said that standing up all day on the concrete floor made his legs and feet ache.

There were windows through which I watched large numbers of men and women sitting at bench-like tables. On the bench was a small machine, which seemed to bend a flat piece of metal into a right angle each time the operator kicked forward a foot lever which hung beneath the bench. No one spoke. They just sat there, eyes focused on the pinchers and repeated the process. Insert, kick, remove; insert, kick, remove. My mother said that talking was not allowed in the shop. She said that if you were seen talking too often, the timekeeper would send you home. My father said that was also true at Winchester. Both of my parents said that since people were paid by the number of pieces of work that passed through their hands each day (piece work), few people stopped work just to talk to someone.

Power presses were activated by a button alongside the machine. The stamping and bending were done with tons of pressure. These were called power presses that were used to stamp, bend, or shape heavier pieces of metal. Again, nobody talked while doing these jobs; they merely sat with their eyes fixed upon the place where the machines delivered their lightning blows. Of all the machines I learned about, the power press remains most vivid in my mind because it was on a power press that my mother lost the tips of three fingers.

I remember one day sitting crouched on my heels looking into the heavy, metal-screened windows at a huge machine which, to me, seemed to be fire polishing brilliant brass doorknobs. The knobs came through a glowing tiny door at the top of the machine through which a metal conveyor belt ran. In soldier-like fashion, the doorknobs came down the conveyor belt, made a turn in front of the window and continued on out of sight. There was a smell of burning grease, as well as tremendous heat that blew in my face through the open window. Then a little partially baldheaded man left the machine where he was standing and came to the window to look out. Except for a heavy canvas apron that covered the central portion of his chest and his lower sides, the man was bare from the waist up.

Hair covered his burly arms, chest, and parts of his back which gleamed with sweat. Atop his forehead was a large pair of clear, plastic goggles. He smiled at me through the window, and said, "Hey, Guyo (hey, boy), you wanna work?" I just peered at him, and he repeated, "You wanna work?" Above the odor of heat and grease and metal, I could smell his perspiration. Then he turned to face the machine once again.

During supper that night, when I told my father about the man's comments to me, he smiled but was visibly upset. "Not my honey boy," he said. "We want you to go to school, learn. You don't want to be like the rest of us. We're working hard so you won't have to do what we're doing."

After supper, while my father took his usual after-dinner nap and my mother and I listened to our favorite weekly radio programs, my mother amplified my father's comments. Again, I cannot remember my age, but I know I was old enough to understand what she was saying. She talked about how much she disliked going to work, especially in the summer when it was so hot in the factory that people passed out while operating the machines. As she described her job to me, she pointed to the little red spots that covered her arms and that portion of her chest between the top of her breastbone to the base of her throat. There were tiny burns from flying hot chips of metal ejected from the machine. She stroked my head as she talked and, as usual, I was aware of the almost sandpaper-like calluses that covered her fingers. The lines and creases that normally covered a person's hands, on my mother were accented by indelibly ground-in grease and grime. Her hands, too, were spotted with red marks from which tiny brass slivers had been plucked.

My mother explained that she and my father worked hard because they wanted my brother and me "to go to school and get an education so that you won't have to work in the shops (i.e., factories) like we do. Daddy gets mad when you talk about looking in the windows of the shops because he hates to think of you inside one of them." Between their collective 95 years of work experience, they had operated all manner of light machinery. At night, usually during dinner, I would tell my father about my daily adventures in machine watching. From my descriptions of the machines and what they appeared to be doing, he would name them and tell me more about how they worked.

At the same time, my father warned me about failing in school. He would say, "Okay, your Mother and I are doing all we can to see that you don't follow our footsteps. But, if you don't shape up, you'll be sweeping streets for the city."

> "You'll be unloading bananas for Williams."
> "You'll be lugging beef for Wilson's."
> "You'll be unloading freight cars."
> "You'll be packing hot dogs for Sperry's."

Before my life turned around, I did each one of these jobs and many others as well.

Nevertheless, I was aware of the inescapable fact that parents throughout the community who worked a variety of menial jobs hoped their children would "go to school, learn and get a better start in life." It was clear to me, even at that age, that parents were sacrificing themselves so that their children could take advantage of their sacrifice and make something of themselves. Most memorable were the special celebrations when my parents shared a glass of wine and toasted that one of them had gotten a five-cent-an-hour wage increase. One common belief in my parents' generation was that an essential part of the American Dream was a steady job by which parents supported their families.

Often the children did not take advantage of the opportunities which their parents tried to provide. For me, it was worse. My reputation as a troubled child was not limited to my activities in the classroom. I hung out with a friend whose reputation was much worse than mine. Moe was always in trouble with the police. One day we were smoking cigarette tobacco in a corn-cob pipe behind a garage. We broke into the garage by pulling loose bricks out of the wall. We made a hole large enough to crawl into the garage. It was dark inside, but Moe found a can of gasoline and spread some gas on the corners of a cement bag, attempting to make a candle. When he lit a match to light this makeshift candle, the vaporized gasoline had already filled the room with gas fumes. We were both lucky. The explosion blew me out of the hole we made in the back wall. Moe scrambled behind me. The front doors blew apart and hung there while the inside roof of the garage began to burn. We ran as the neighbors were screaming. The fire department came. There was black smoke everywhere. The fire was quickly put out. The police were called, and we were caught. The car in the garage was not burned. The only damage was to the front doors and the tarred roof. But that was it. The neighborhood parents, who named me "Crazy Mikey," would not allow their children to play with me any longer. That was fine with me. Moe and I had other friends who, like me, were also ostracized. Throughout those early years, Moe and I remained friends. Eventually, he was sent to prison and, sadly, died of Hodgkin's lymphoma.

Amid the flurry of criticisms directed at me during those early teen years, my mother, grandmother, and Aunt Mary stood by me, always encouraging me to try harder. Along with them was my guitar teacher, Frank D'Amato, an accomplished musician who played banjo in the thirties and guitar in the forties. In those days, Broadway shows debuted in the Schubert Theater in New Haven, and Mr. D'Amato was always in the orchestra pit.

I began guitar lessons when I was 13. Mr. D'Amato told me that I had the talent to become a professional musician but that I had to stay in school and receive a diploma. He was constantly trying to help me. He could not understand how I could be so disciplined as a music student and so undisciplined in the rest of my life. Of all the people who tried to help me in those troubled years, Mr. D'Amato was the most important. He constantly told me that school was first and the guitar was second; that I would never be successful as a musician without an education.

My brother was also in trouble in his early years. He was my step-brother whose mother died in childbirth. Unable to care for him, my father placed baby Anthony with the parents of his first wife. They blamed my father for the death of their daughter and punished my brother by locking him in a cellar during his childhood. After my father married my mother and I was born, eleven-year-old Anthony came to live with us. My mother loved him but understood that he was an extremely troubled child. As he grew into his teens, he became violent, constantly in fights where police were called to arrest him. When I was a child, I became aware of his violent reputation and was present when my father had him removed from our apartment by the riot squad. In his twenties, he became a union enforcer who prevented non-member drivers from delivering trailers into union yards. My parents feared that he would one day be killed on the job.

Yet there was another side to him. He played the chromatic harmonica. Not folk tunes, but show tunes and classical music. He could not read a note but was able to play famous violin pieces such as the "Hora Staccato" and the "Romanian Rhapsody" as perfectly as did internationally celebrated harmonica virtuoso Larry Adler. Yet Tony's talent went largely unrecognized.

My brother and I played popular music at weddings and exclusive country resorts like Pine Orchard Country Club in the New Haven area. He played so well that under the name Tony Zane he served as a spokesman for the Hohner Harmonica Company, a German musical instrument maker that was the only producer of chromatic harmonicas used by noted virtuosos who played classical music.

Another side of this complicated young man was that he was an insatiable reader of philosophy. Despite not having completed middle school, he read Plato, Aristotle, Marx, Hegel, and Nietzsche. Unlike me, he could read a page as fast as he could turn it. He and his wife, who helped him change his violent behavior, were the parents of four children.

My father was distraught and saddened when, after years of poor study habits and complete lack of interest, my brother quit school. My brother faced the inevitable problems of those without a high school diploma. Attempting to influence me, my parents tried to use the difficulties confronting my brother as an example to motivate me to remain in school. But their efforts proved to be in vain when, at 16 years of age, two weeks after I enrolled at Wilbur Cross High School, I quit.

Reading this book as a parent, you may not be faced with a child exhibiting antisocial behaviors that sometimes mask a child's hidden problems. Sometimes the symptom may be isolation or shying away from the company of other kids. You would also want to watch the friends they keep. My parents were uneducated. They did what they could to understand my problems, yet they were unable to help me stay in school. You may be well-educated working parents who may not have the time to monitor your children or know of the double lives they may lead. You must take the time and know what your children are doing when you are not around. I would encourage you to do as much as you can to help your children. The key is to be watchful and mindful.

Chapter 2

Out of School—A Job A Week

Anyone looking at my educational history would know that leaving school early in life was inevitable. Both my parents left school before middle school. In the 1920s, children of working-class families went to work to support the family. This was especially true during the Great Depression.

As a teenager and still in school, I was always able to find a job where I worked for a few hours and was paid for helping local merchants unload trucks. Local fruit peddlers would travel to markets where wholesalers loaded their trucks to the point of overflowing. When the merchants returned to their local stores and warehouses, they paid teenagers to unload those trucks. There were several merchants who dealt in bananas. Trucks were loaded in New York with green bananas coming from South America in bunches still on the stalks cut from a tree. The stalks ranged in size from four to five feet in length and were extremely heavy. Each bunch was handed from the truck to a waiting teenager who carried that bunch down a flight of stairs to a room where the ceiling was covered with hooks. There, a man on a ladder would take the hemp rope from around the bunch and affix it to a hook on the ceiling. When all the hooks were filled, we moved to another room to continue the process until all the rooms were filled and the truck emptied. Some of the smaller dealers would warehouse only twenty or thirty bunches of bananas. Larger dealers would empty an entire trailer with several hundred bunches. It was hard work that demanded teenagers like me who had physical strength.

Retail merchants in the area also hired teenagers to unload heavy boxes of tomatoes, olives, and artichokes—either canned or bottled—in cartons of twelve to twenty. Again, the containers were extremely heavy; only the strongest teenagers were hired. All of these jobs provided school-aged youngsters with spending money for dates, movies, etc. However, these jobs could not be classified as "steady" employment.

Even while in middle school, some teenagers in our neighborhood made money on Sunday when dice games were held at the basement below a coffee shop or in the cellar of someone's home. We parked and washed the Cadillacs, Oldsmobiles, and Packards of the gamblers. Those who won paid us as much as $20 per car. Those who lost did not pay us, and we did not ask for money. It was easy to identify the winners who were joyfully smiling and whose hands were filled with $20 and $50 bills. The losers were somber, empty handed, and often exhibited expressions of anger. The dice games played in our working-class neighborhood attracted wealthy, impulsive gamblers drawn to the action in these tenement basements. One frequent player was the son and heir to the fortune of one of Connecticut's largest manufacturing companies.

For a short time, I worked setting up pins in a bowling alley. In those days there were no machines to set up pins. I had a problem holding the pins between my fingers. My guitar teacher counseled against my taking any job that would damage my fingers. I realized that others who set up pins regularly had fingers that were distorted. Since I wanted to be a professional guitarist I quit because that job would have left me unable to play guitar.

Once out of school, I needed to find a fulltime job. Walking through the marketplace downtown a man called to me, "Hey kid. You want a job?" Moments later, I was wearing an apron, waiting on customers buying vegetables at the market. I ran into an immediate problem. I was unable to determine the cost of a purchase. If the customer wanted two or three pounds of something that had a fixed price per pound, I could manage. But when the scale showed a fraction of a pound, I could not compute the cost. Once the purchase was made, I could not make change. The basic arithmetic required for making change or determining the cost of a fraction of a pound made it impossible for me to wait on customers. I was reassigned to bringing boxes of vegetables up from the basement. Again, grunt work. A few days later I was let go.

I then tried my hand at factory work. I was hired as a trucker, a job with a misleading title. A trucker carries or drags filled boxes of tiny parts from one machine to another where the workers performed various operations on the parts. Not only was this job tiring, it was boring because none of the machine operators would stop to talk to me. Once again, I was let go. I became a trucker in a few other companies, but the results were the same. I was always let go because I was distracting workers.

I took a job as an apprentice candy maker at the Mary Oliver Candy Company. My job was to take a small canoe paddle and stir boiling hot kettles of glucose. Each batch of glucose became the mix that created lollipops. I enjoyed learning how taffy, fudge, and chocolate-covered cherry candies were made, but I did not get along with another employee. We were both fired for fighting and disrupting the kitchen. I told the manager I was innocent because the other apprentice started the argument. But I was fired anyway. In anger, before leaving the kitchen, I pulled the large rubber mold containing sugar bunnies, decapitating the bunnies being prepared for Easter delivery to local shops.

I was hired by the Brewster Shirt Company, a fairly large neighborhood garment factory producing shirts for shipments to outlets in the Northeast and mid-Atlantic states. That same shirt that one buys neatly folded and pinned in place and wrapped plastic begins with a roll of material that is laid down and spread on a 100-foot table, one layer at a time. In my job description, I was termed a "spreader." I was intrigued about how serious the chief spreader took his job. He would take the end of a sheet of material from a huge bolt of cloth mounted on a spool at the end of the table and walk ceremoniously down the length of the table. The spreaders, like me, followed using our hands to remove any wrinkles that appeared in the fabric. This process continued layer after layer. As each layer was smoothed down, the material piled into a stack five to seven inches high.

When the rolls of material were exhausted, a paper pattern was placed on top of the stack. Then a master cutter with a jigsaw-like electric knife cut the material on the table into fronts, backs, sleeves, collars, etc. When the cutter had cut the fabrics beneath the pattern, my job was to tie each of the cut sections together with string, put them in a large basket, and wheel them downstairs to the floor below where women sewed the parts into a complete shirt.

It was here that I first experienced the reality of a sweat shop. There were scores of women in an un-air-conditioned room filled with the odor of machine oil and perspiration. By mid-summer, the heat in the sewing room was nearing 100 degrees. The large fans moved the odor around the room but did not lower the temperature. Once I delivered the cut fabrics to the sewing room, I had to begin spreading the next bolts of cloth. The other boys working at Brewster's were always clowning around. We would use the long cardboard cones on which the material was wound as sabers hitting each other on the head. The managers were not amused.

The shop overlooked Water Street. One day I looked down on the street below and saw friends with towels hitchhiking to the beach. All I could think of was how many years the head spreader worked as a spreader before he was promoted. I said to myself, 'not me,' and right after lunch I walked off the job, picked up a towel at my house a block away, and followed my friends to the beach. As I left the shop that day, I couldn't help noticing my fellow spreaders, some married men with children, looking at me as I left. The freedom I had to just quit whenever I wanted was something they all envied.

From that point on a pattern was set. I was hired or fired and sometimes I accepted a job and never showed up for work. For example, I was once hired to wear a four-foot-high peanut shell, black top hat and a cane, and a black leotard leggings with additional arm sleeves. I was to be Mr. Peanut. My job was to parade in front of a peanut store amid the smell of freshly roasted peanuts blowing out of the storefront into the street. I told the employer of my concern of being identified. He assured me that no one would know who was in the peanut shell costume. Over that weekend, I reconsidered the offer. What would my friends think when they found out I was Mr. Peanut? The next Monday I did not show up for work.

For a short time, I worked lugging beef from a refrigerated freight car into a refrigerated warehouse where the meat was cut into those sections one finds in a local supermarket or a butcher shop. I was absolutely amazed when the door on the freight car opened and I saw what was hanging from large hooks in the ceiling of the railcar. It was a cow cut into four pieces—two forequarters and two hindquarters, each weighing nearly 200 pounds. To carry a forequarter, you had to put your fingers between the jagged ribs cut with a power saw. You hooked the leg of the forearm with a steel hook then got under the forequarter and lifted it from the hook back onto your chest. Then you walked over the narrow steel plate between the railcar and the loading dock. On the dock, overhead was a conveyor belt where you would lift the beef up onto a hook that carried it away. Then you returned to the railcar to repeat the process until the car was empty.

The jagged edges of the rib bones would slice your fingers. All I could think of was cutting my fingers and not being able to practice my guitar lessons. The manager said I could wear gloves, but that didn't help. The jagged edges of the ribs cut right through the gloves. When I threatened to quit, they offered me a job in the ham division where I would assist an old Polish immigrant who deboned hams with a knife. He was very encouraging and said I could replace him when he retired. My job was to take the deboned ham and, using a press, squeeze the ham into a stainless-steel box and lower it into a giant vat where the hams were boiled. When it emerged from the hot water it looked like loaves of boiled ham that you see in the meat department of a supermarket. I then had to clean the vats where the hams were boiled. Again, the risk of cutting my guitar fingers on the steel boxes led me to quit.

I then applied for a job with another meat packer as a ham smoker. Again, movement of hams was facilitated by tracks on the ceiling that held metal racks called "ham trees." Each rack held from twenty to thirty hams wrapped in a cloth stocking. Once the trees were filled, they were moved to what appeared to be an elevator shaft without the elevator. The ham trees were rolled into a room with a metal grate floor through which one could see similar floors above and below. When each of the floors in this elevator shaft were filled with ham trees, the manager and I went to the basement where two large gas jets were lit and covered with hickory sawdust. The fire did not burn, it smoldered sending smoke up through the floors above. The hams were smoked for twenty-four hours. The manager went into the room to periodically test the internal temperature of selected hams.

Here's the good part. I had to accompany my supervisor into that smoke-filled room where breathing was almost impossible. Taking temperatures of the hams on the top floor was challenging enough because it was the hottest place in the elevator shaft. But when I went down to the floors below, the hot fat dripped down on me from the melting fat on the hams above. I had already developed a reputation as a wise guy and was warned by my boss not to make enemies at the facility. "All you need is for someone to slam that door shut while you were taking temperatures, and no one would know you were there for the next twenty-four hours. You would come out Wilson certified."

Once the hams were removed from the trees, the job got worse. I was to take a steam hose to each of the floor grates to wash the fat down to the basement.

Finally, I had to steam clean the floor of the fat and hickory dust from the floors above. I managed to get through two weeks and then quit.

Knowing of my experience in meat processing, my cousin Frankie, an office manager, recommended me for a job at Sperry & Barnes, a company that processed pork ribs and shoulders and made hotdogs. Frankie told me, unlike lugging beef, we would be dealing with processing small units that were not at all heavy. I reported for work at 6:00 a.m. the next Monday. I was fitted with a large yellow rain slicker, pants with straps, and boots up to my thighs. I was brought down into a sub-basement by an elevator where I faced a door with steam seeping under the door frame. A very nice black man met me there and tried to assure me that I would do just fine in this job. We entered a steam-filled room that had a large conveyor belt on the ceiling. I could barely breathe, and my eyeglasses were clouded with fog. Suddenly I heard blood curdling screams. Pigs were being killed on the other side of the wall and hung on a conveyor belt that moved along the ceiling into our room where we were to wash them with steam coming from our hoses. I dropped the hose and ran for the door. The black man followed me out the door saying that once the initial shock was over, I'd be just fine. I responded, "I will never be fine," and could never enter that room again.

I asked to see my cousin Frankie right then and there. Frankie came down to see what was wrong. I told him I was ready to quit. He said, "You're crazy. You're making $2.25 an hour, which is one of the highest rates in the company!" He told me he would find another place for me in the company.

My new job was to be in the pickling department trucking hams and pork shoulders to large vats of ice-cold pickle where they waited to be cut, ground, and made into sausage or hotdogs. My cousin, knowing of my quick temper, warned me not to antagonize anyone in the shop, noting that a few weeks earlier, a knife was thrown between two workers, an artery was severed, and a worker died before he could get to a hospital only a few blocks away.

In this new position, I was escorted into a refrigerated room where men and women were injecting preservative pickle juice into the hams and pork shoulders. I was freezing. I couldn't feel my fingers. Everyone in that room had arthritis in their hands. I was studying to be a guitarist. I knew that was no place for me. Frankie asked me to be patient and give it a week. "A week?" I quit right after lunch. When I was being processed out, one of the human resources managers told me the other H.R. officials were taking bets on how long I would last. They weren't even close. They were betting a week or two. I was out by 1:00 p.m., one half day after I started. After this episode, my reputation in the family was now seriously damaged. Not even my own family members would help me find another job.

One summer I was offered the opportunity to work for Barnum Machine & Tool Company, one of the machine shops that serviced oil tankers on the waterfront. They were located on Wooster Street, around the corner from my home. My job was to shovel out metal chips that collected in open trays beneath the cutting blades of the different machines. On one machine, called a boring mill, the chips collected in a chamber below the machine. That chamber was illuminated by one light bulb. As I shoveled the oil-soaked chips through the little hatch-like door into a wheelbarrow, within minutes I was soaked with sweat and was exhausted. While I was resting on the shovel, breathing heavily, I heard the old machinist laughing as he peered at me through the hatch. "You're not tired already are you, sonny?" asked the little but heavily muscled man with gray hair as he clutched the stem of his corncob pipe tightly between his teeth.

"There's not enough air in here, and the chips are soaked with oil. They're really heavy," I responded.

"Heavy," said the old man removing the pipe from his mouth. "You don't know what heavy is. Why, I had to shovel those chips for years before I even got to be a machinist helper."

Looking back now, Barnum was a great opportunity to become a machinist. There were only three machinists in the shop—a Frenchman, a German, and a Swede.

As I wandered through the shop, I was fascinated with the different machines and techniques used for cutting, bending, and drilling different kinds of metal. I watched those master machinists rubbing their grease-stained hands over a shaft or valve feeling for a thousandth of an inch variable. Only later in life did I appreciate the knowledge I obtained from those machinists even in the few weeks that I worked at Barnum. I was let go because my job was to shovel chips, not observe the machinists at work. But the work and skills of those machinists stayed forever fixed in my mind. Today, I realize that those skilled craftsmen are a dying breed of worker without which America's industrial base cannot survive. No other job that I held during my teenaged years had such a lasting impact on me as did Barnum Machine Company.

I did not appear to be cut out for indoor work. There was another choice, however, and that was to enter one of the skilled trades. But, once again, it was far more demanding of the individual than that of being a common laborer. It required years of hard work at low wages. It also required discipline and humility on the part of the apprentice who, being the lowest man on the ladder, had to do all of the grunt work. In that first year after leaving school, I entered a number of trades, all of which I abandoned within days—and in some cases hours—simply because I had neither the patience, nor humility, to withstand the job requirements. I lacked both experience and knowledge. I was horrified to discover that to be a carpenter's apprentice I had to carry boards for the carpenters or be sent to fetch this or that tool when it was needed. "Hey, kid. Get that crosscut saw from the truck. I said a crosscut saw! Not a ripsaw, you damn dummy!"

I soon left the carpenter apprenticeship, but it was just as bad in all the other trades I tried. I refused to carry wire for the licensed electrician, the bricks, cinderblocks or mortar for the master mason, or the pipes for the plumber. I left all these jobs in disgust. I was tired of being ordered to, "Go get this; go get that; carry this; clean up that." I was angry at the way I was being treated.

Some of the neighborhood dropouts did enter the trades, and after years of low wages, hard work, and sacrifice they became master tradesmen respected by the community and well paid for their work. The point is that never did I nor any of my friends begrudge those who had earned a better station in life. All of us who did not have the patience, humility, or were just too lazy to put out the effort recognized that we had no one to blame but ourselves for having walked away from the opportunity to learn a trade. In a sense, we had also earned our station in life.

Again, I recall the neighborhood comments about those who earned higher wages and the respect of the community.

"He worked for years in the hot sun and freezing cold carrying boards up ladders. Today he is a carpenter."

"I remember when he used to come home looking like a snowman covered in plaster and concrete from head to toe. Today he gives the orders and others do the work."

"He had grooves in his shoulders from years of carrying pipes. He used to come home with his clothes and shoes soaked with water from broken toilet pipes. He stank from head to toe. Today he owns his own company."

"For years before he owned that garage, he used to change oil, grease cars, and fix flat tires. Today he barely gets his hands dirty."

The willingness to accept success or failure as the individual's responsibility was the touchstone of our community. The young people in our area learned from their own parents and from the parents of others that in America opportunity was placed within your reach. My immigrant grandmother frequently told me that in America the streets were lined with gold, but you have to bend down to pick it up. I learned from her that if you truly wanted to better yourself, nothing would stop you. If you made only a half-hearted effort or waited for someone else to do it for you, failure was guaranteed. Young people in our neighborhood were taught and believed that— barring sickness or accident—hard work, sacrifice, individual responsibility, merit, and success were all found together.

My father, who had only two jobs in his entire life, was most upset by my serial failures in employment. My mother worked at Sargent Hardware Company her entire life. They were embarrassed that I could not hold a single job. I remember the accountant who helped my parents file their income tax once saying to me as he looked at a stack of my W-2 forms that looked like a deck of cards, "Should we cut the deck before we start?"

Following my quitting school, every activity I engaged in reflected a total lack of common sense. Since my parents never owned an automobile, my brother helped me buy a car by putting the car in his name. It was a 1941 Ford that was constantly being repaired. When the repair bills became outrageous, I convinced my mother to co-sign a loan to buy a new 1953 Dodge. Like many teenagers, I was addicted to driving fast and going through caution lights. I had numerous accidents. Within a few short years the only side of the car that was undamaged was the driver's side door. When my auto insurance was canceled, I could only be covered by going through the Connecticut state assigned risk pool for drivers who had a reason for submitting too many claims. Being totally irresponsible I did not service the car properly and ran it hard between oil changes. I often refused to add engine oil when the gas station attendants told me the oil was down about a quart. When the car seemed to run just fine with a quart low, I stretched it to two quarts before I added oil. Eventually the engine threw a piston through the head and the car had to be junked, leaving me with a debt of $1,200 and no car. My abuse of the car mirrored my disrespect for the work ethic as well.

From what has been said thus far, it should be apparent that, with respect to the work ethic, the philosophical overview of the neighborhood ethnic groups stood flatly in the tradition of the American experience. But hard work and sacrifice were only part of the success equation. To have the motivation for advancement was necessary to be sure, but, beyond that, one also had to have a political system that afforded its citizens the opportunity for economic and social advancement. The ethnic groups in our neighborhood knew only too well that, in their native countries, that desire for economic and social mobility was meaningless, because the social and political systems in those countries did not provide for upward mobility.

MY MILITARY SERVICE

In 1950 the Korean War began. Early in the conflict, the Connecticut National Guard, one of the first military units sent to Korea, suffered major casualties. By 1953, when I was turning 18, the War had turned into a major conflict. Many young men in the neighborhood were being drafted into the Army and were serving in Korea. That was when a friend convinced me to join the Connecticut National Guard. The word was out that, if you joined the Guard, you would not be drafted because Connecticut was trying to rebuild the Guard. I joined the Guard with other neighborhood friends, viewing it like school—if we didn't like it, we could always quit. We met once a week and were expected to spend two weeks on active duty. Once we were sworn in, it was clear that quitting was not possible.

My behavior on drill night mirrored what I exhibited in school. I was a nuisance--laughing, joking, and generally disrupting the lectures. To me it was just like grade school and middle school. I was removed from the class and disciplined by Captain Russo. I told the Captain I did not really enjoy the

Guard and was thinking of quitting. Captain Russo responded that he did not think I understood the seriousness of my decision to join the Guard. He told me that I could not quit and that if he threw me out, I would be subject to immediate induction into the regular Army. He also said he could give me a dishonorable discharge, adding I would never get a job with the word *dishonorable* attached to my record. I was convinced it was time to keep my mouth shut and serve my two years. After all, it was only one night a week. I was in the medical corps and we constantly practiced dressing wounds and splinting broken legs. I always offered to be splinted so I didn't have to do anything but lay there. Besides, I was still free to hold a daytime job.

Intent on becoming a serious guitar player, I moved to Miami, Florida, where I could play Latin music. I moved down there with a close friend of my family, Mary Scarpellino, who owned the apartment in whose bedroom I was born. Trying to help me, she invited me to stay with her family in Florida and see if I could find a job there to get myself straightened out. Soon after, the hired-fired-quit process began all over again.

I worked at a supermarket trimming produce in the vegetable section, for a housing development cutting sod blocks with a machete along with early Cuban refugees running from the dictatorial regime of Fulgencio Batista, and on construction sites moving lumber and drainpipes. I also worked in a lounge chair factory packing boxes with chaise lounges. I mistakenly packed lounges marked "white" and "white-white" in the same boxes when their colors were slightly different. The manager of the factory was furious. He told me the chairs that I packed were shipped in boxes marked "white." My response was, "What the hell, they're all white aren't they?" I was fired that day.

I worked as a busboy at one of Miami's largest yacht clubs. I was let go because I fought with another busboy who kept taking coffee from my stand rather than getting his own from the kitchen. As our argument grew louder, I threatened to throw a pot of coffee at him. He hid behind the diners at his table who were terrified they would be hit with a flying pot of hot coffee. The maître d' came upon the scene in the middle of the argument. I tried to tell him the other busboy was stealing my coffee. He would not listen and fired me on the spot. I ripped off my waiter's jacket and walked bare-chested through the dining room to my car parked in the lot.

I stacked shelves at a large supermarket called Food Fair. I was let go because I stamped the sale price from the week before on the current shelves. The manager was very nice. He said, "You know, Mike. Some people are better off being a truck driver. There are other things that you might be able to do. This is not one of them." I took a job driving a large dump truck and was fired because I backed into a swamp sinking half the truck in the muddy water.

When I first moved to Florida, I transferred from the Connecticut National Guard to the Florida National Guard. Captain Russo was glad to see me go and sent my transfer papers to Captain Piper in Florida. When I arrived in Florida, I checked in with Captain Piper who let me know that he had heard of me from Captain Russo and hoped I would do well there. But in Florida, as in Connecticut, I was the class clown on drill nights. Worse still, I was eroding the morale of the entire unit. I was seen as a troublemaking northerner who constantly collided with the non-commissioned officers and the enlisted men.

On one occasion, Captain Piper spoke with me about the seriousness of being in the guard. He was a decent guy who—except for me—ran a cohesive unit. I told him I would do my best to improve.

The major event for the Florida National Guard was the annual inspection made by a general from the regular army. Captain Piper told the assembly a week earlier that this was the most important event for the unit. We were to arrive two hours early on the night of the general's review so that Captain Piper could conduct a mock review himself well before the general arrived. He made it clear that he and the general would want to see their faces in the mirror-shine on our boots. I had been working on construction that week and wore my uniform on the job site. My shoes and clothes were coated in cement dust. When I arrived, the inspection had already started. My unit had already closed ranks, so there was no room in the place where I normally stood. I walked along the lines looking for a place to fall-in.

As I moved through the ranks, I remember the smell of simonize car wax, a smell generated by the wax on the boots to give them a mirrored finish that Captain Piper requested. My movement through the ranks became noticeable because, except for the general and Captain Piper reviewing the troops, I was the only soldier moving through the ranks. When I could find no place to stand, I simply stood at the end of one of the lines. It made the unit uneven but at least I was there. Looking back at it now, it would have been better if I had not attended the inspection. But it was too late.

Suddenly, the general was in front of me. I stood at attention while he looked at me. As he looked at my

- 50 -

plaster-covered uniform and cement-covered boots, the smell of shoe polish on the boots of all the other soldiers appeared more prominent. Captain Piper stood looking at me with laser eyes as the general asked if I was aware that my uniform was totally unacceptable for an announced inspection. I told him that, since I did not have work clothes, I wore my combat fatigues and dress boots on the construction site. He turned and faced Captain Piper and said something to the Captain that I could not hear. The Captain nodded and said, "Yes sir, I will take care of that." Captain Piper never spoke with me again, but my 1st Sergeant said that when we went off to fulltime bivouac that summer, they were going to kill me.

After my having lost so many jobs in Florida, Mary's patience was beginning to wear out. I returned to Connecticut, but I did not bother checking in with the Connecticut National Guard for several months. When I finally met with Captain Russo, I found him very happy. He told me that too much time had elapsed since my transfer from Florida, and that my transfer papers never arrived. He said that technically I was AWOL in both states and could be subjected to immediate induction into the regular army. I asked Captain Russo if he could fix this for me. He laughed and said, "Are you kidding? Both Captain Piper and I believe you are an insult to the military and we're moving you out."

He said Captain Piper had told him the only reason I was not court-martialed over the inspection was because the general was told I was a mental case that Captain Piper was committed to removing from the military.

As far as Connecticut was concerned, I was AWOL and now available for immediate induction. When I asked for another chance, Captain Russo told me that two of my friends in the Guard were now in jail, that he finally had a cohesive unit, and for me to get out. As I opened the door to leave, he shouted, "Balzano!" I turned thinking he had changed his mind. "You're no damn good! The trouble with you is that you are a born leader, but you lead men in the wrong direction. If you ever straightened yourself out," he said, "you would be one hell of a citizen. Now get out." In fact, Russo was very kind to me. He could have given me a dishonorable discharge, which would have followed me all my life. As it turned out, decades later I was to advise six United States Presidents, three Secretaries of Defense, and several three-star and four-star generals and admirals, as well as members of the Joint Chiefs.

WORKING FOR THE DEPARTMENT OF SANITATION

Once back in Connecticut my reputation for being fired or quitting a job made it impossible for me to find anyone to hire me in New Haven. My mother took me to the home of a local Don.[3] Previously he helped my brother get a job at the New Haven Department of Sanitation as a garbage and refuse collector. He offered me the same option. When I questioned it, I was told this was it. Take it or leave it. I joined my brother on the garbage truck. My brother and I worked well together. We faced the elements, cold, snowy, rainy, winter days, and steaming hot summers. Often on rainy days we were covered with ashes from coal-burning furnaces where ashes were in cans or thirty-gallon drums along the street.

In the summer, people put garbage in the bottom of the can, and it spilled down into our sleeves. Every summer my arms would break out with boils that had to be lanced. My doctor could not identify the kind of infection, but suspected it came from bacteria in the garbage cans. When our work was done, we showered at the city supply house or the YMCA. I really hated the job, but the hours were convenient for practicing the guitar. We began the garbage collecting route at midnight and finished often before nine in the morning. With the exception of my friends and family, no one knew I was a garbage collector.

The job did have an advantage: it provided me with the time to practice guitar and rehearse with the different bands that I played with on weekends. During the summers I had time to go to the beach. I thought I would be a professional musician. Everything seemed fine, but my life was about to change suddenly. Somehow, I lifted a trash can the wrong way. My back went out and I was left in excruciating pain. The early diagnosis was that I had ruptured a disc in my spine. Wisely, my doctor told me not to have surgery of any kind, but to wait it out. I was told not to bend or lift anything weighing more than a pound. The obvious thought that went through my mind was that I was already mentally disabled and earned a living with a strong back. Now I was physically disabled as well. My career as a garbage man ended.

That weekend I played a job at a country club. Ray Boffa, the drummer in the band, saw me struggling to lift my amplifier from the trunk of my car. He picked it up and brought it into the bandstand. When the job was over, Ray and I talked. I told him I was in deep trouble, that I couldn't lift anything heavier than a pound. How would I make a living? Ray was known in the neighborhood as a good kid. He graduated from high school, played local baseball, and was never associated with anyone who could be called "bad." Even though we had played in several bands together, Ray did not really know me, but he took a sincere interest in me. He shared that he worked for the American Optical Company and had the opportunity to hire someone for a job that had just opened within the company. He told me he was close to completing the apprenticeship requirements for becoming a licensed optician, and he thought I could follow in his footsteps. I said, "Ray, you don't understand. I'm stupid. I failed at every trade I tried. I can't do basic arithmetic, and I can barely read and write."

Ray put his hand on my shoulder and said, "Mike, you're a smart guy. You read music. You play a mean guitar. You can't be stupid. The job pays forty-cents an hour. You will be an apprentice lens grinder like I am. I will monitor your work. I will help you."

I nodded and said, "Okay. I'll try."

Parents reading this chapter may want to take note of the number of jobs that I had during those first years after I quit school. My behavior was abnormal, to be sure. But it should also be noted that most of the jobs I had and lost were jobs that did not require me to read anything. Nor did they require any serious contemplation on my part. They required only physical strength—all I thought I had to offer. I now realize that I was unconsciously hiding academic weaknesses that I had accumulated over my school years. By monitoring the patterns their children develop, parents may see behaviors that mask more serious problems. It is also important to try to identify where their children's strengths lie. I had developed some very poor patterns of behavior; but, at the same time, it was clear—to someone like Ray, at least—that I was capable of learning when I wanted to. I was also capable of discipline when it came to studying the guitar.

- 55 -

to. I was also capable of discipline when it came to studying the guitar.

Chapter 3

An Apprenticeship:
My Road to Recovery

When I told Ray I would accept the job he offered, deep inside I knew I would let him down. I did not believe I had the intelligence to understand directions or the ability to perform the simplest tasks that might be required of me. Even so, I met Ray on the following Monday morning at a branch office of the American Optical Company in downtown New Haven. Ray introduced me to a small staff of professional craftsmen who operated a wholesale optical laboratory. Optometrists and retail optical stores in the New Haven area phoned in prescriptions to the American Optical lab, and the staff ground and fitted lenses into frames supplied by the retail customers. The staff delivered a finished product ready to be dispensed at a fitting table in an optical store or doctor's office.

Ray explained that I would become registered in an apprenticeship operated by the State of Connecticut Optical Commission. The Commission consisted of licensed opticians who worked in retail optical stores throughout the state. The apprenticeship required that an apprentice serve in four areas: surface grinding, cutting and mounting finished lenses into an optical frame, measuring and fitting glasses to the patient, and optical theory. The process took at least four years, but many people spent years in one phase and never moved on to complete the requirements for an optical license.

In the early days, retail optical houses had labs on the premises where technicians ground lenses for the patients who came to the optical store. Over time, it became difficult for retail labs to train lens grinders, who expected to be promoted to other phases of the work, to become fully licensed as opticians themselves. There were two major wholesale optical companies in the Northeast that sold supplies to optical retailers: American Optical and Bausch & Lomb. They also supplied finished lenses to retailers where simple prescriptions were cut and mounted into a patient's eyeglass frame or one supplied by the optical store. They also supplied unfinished opaque lenses one-half to three-quarters of an inch thick that had to be ground on both sides. At American Optical, our task was to grind both sides of the lens to produce the curves on the lens that coincided with the prescription written by the ophthalmologist.

Ray introduced me to the starting point in the process. My job was to fit a glass blank onto a metal wafer by heating a material that adhered the metal to the glass. The wafer held the lens in place throughout the grinding process. With Ray constantly looking over my shoulder, despite my concerns, I performed the task well. A month into that operation, Ray moved me to the grinding phase where I was cutting glass. A few months later, he moved me to the surfacing and polishing of glass to the specifics required by the prescription.

The most senior craftsman on the staff was a man named Adolph whose knowledge of optics was legendary. At first, he teased me saying he didn't believe a "spaghetti eater" could become a lens grinder. He constantly remarked that one would have to eat a lot of sauerkraut to really grind lenses, i.e., you had to be German, or Swedish, not Italian. The message was clear: Germans were smart, Italians were stupid.

At first, I was angry and was prepared to do battle with him. This was my old pattern in many of the other jobs that I lost. In the past, I would take a self-defense position and return the insults. Ray overheard Adolph's insults and laughed out loud saying that Adolph had told him that, too. Instead of insulting Adolph or quitting, I simply laughed. In the past I would not let the slightest insult pass. I might have even walked off the job in protest. Adolph never let up, constantly saying I was not qualified. Uncharacteristically, I simply let the insults roll off me. I didn't attack Adolph because of my respect for Ray, who stuck out his neck to hire me. I would not let him down. That was the first time I ever felt obligated to anyone who tried to help me.

Ray explained that Adolph really liked me, or I wouldn't be there. He was the master lens grinder and if he had any hesitation about my ability, I would never be allowed to continue the apprenticeship.

Then one day, Adolph pulled me aside and said I was one of the best surface grinders he had trained. Wow! Not only did I survive for over six months on a job, but the staff actually liked me, and the work I did. Ray said that others were not surprised that Adolph would say what he did because they also saw my work as being excellent.

I remember thinking, *okay I have mastered a series of tasks that required manual skills, and I am proud of what I have accomplished. But those tasks did not require brains. They required mastering the skill I was taught.* Later, something happened that changed my thinking about my ability. I detected errors made in computing curves on the lenses that I ground.

As the lenses passed my operation, I took note of the directions written on the glass and compared them with the numbers written on the prescription. After months of observation, I began to detect errors made by the layout technician. I told Ray the instructions on the lenses were in conflict with the numbers called for on the prescription. Ray looked at me and said, "How do you know that?" I explained that I had developed a formula for computing the curves required on the prescription. Ray told Don Disbrow, the branch manager, who approached me one lunch hour and questioned how I had arrived at the correct numbers. I gave him the formula I created to select the appropriate tool to match the numbers on the prescription. Disbrow looked at me with amazement. "Mike, do you have any idea what you've done? You have deduced a basic formula in algebra that you would have learned in one day of high school math." You really should return to school and get a high school diploma."

Shortly after I began my optical apprenticeship, I married a neighborhood girl whom I had known since grade school. She was a high school graduate and valedictorian of her class. I was still on the garbage truck when we decided to marry. At twenty years old, I was a mess. I had debt amounting to almost two thousand dollars. Having a woman in your life can be a great advantage. She encouraged me to complete the optical apprenticeship and to obtain a high school diploma. She even used her own money to pay off my debts, including my debt on my guitars and on my car. I could not have turned my life around without her help.

I remained at American Optical for two years but realized that to complete the apprenticeship I had to move on to other phases of the work. But there were only so many openings at American Optical, so I applied to one of the oldest and most prestigious retailers in New Haven, the Harvey & Lewis Optical Company. They still ran their own optical lab and ground 90% of the lenses for their patients in-house. The person who ran their optical lab moved up the chain, leaving an opening for someone to run their surface department. I became manager of the department, but I still relied on Ray and Mr. Disbrow for help.

Each day before I reported to work, I went to the American Optical office where Ray taught me the next operation in cutting lenses and fitting them into frames. That operation came only after the finished lenses left the surfacing department. Suddenly, there was an opening at Harvey & Lewis in the next phase for the optical apprenticeship. Because of Ray's help, I was prepared for that assignment and was promoted to the cutting and edging department.

The last phase of the apprenticeship was actually fitting patients. Again, Ray and I practiced on fitting lenses and bifocals with each other. We also studied theory together. In a year, we were both prepared to take the state optical exam.

After my original conversation with Mr. Disbrow concerning my ability to solve math problems without professional instruction, he urged me to return to high school. At the time, the state of Connecticut operated a fulltime high school program at night to help those veterans from the Korean War who held fulltime day jobs. I enrolled in that program and attended classes four nights a week. At first, I was nervous about returning to school, an arena in which I had never succeeded. But since I already had some success in the optical apprenticeship, I thought I would try.

Returning to high school was difficult. I was required to listen to lectures, then read textbooks about the lecture. I began to notice that in reading Shakespeare's Macbeth or Longfellow, words in the text changed places. When the written words did not convey the correct storyline, I simply reread those passages out loud until the message made sense. Obviously, it took more time to read a chapter than any of my other classmates. But that did not bother me because I loved what I was reading.

I remember, while in grammar school, although I failed all the courses, I enjoyed the classes on Greek history. I was especially interested in Greek mythology. When I returned to evening high school, I sought out courses in ancient history. I also took classes in Shakespeare and was fascinated by Macbeth and Hamlet. I even took chemistry. Both working and going to school, over the next four years, I graduated from high school and also received my optical license.

A WIDER CIRCLE OF FRIENDS

From the beginning of my optical apprenticeship, I ran into people who noticed my ability to memorize complex information and believed it was a sign of intelligence. All of them encouraged me to go back to high school. Joe DeBaise was a young Air Force officer who worked with me at Harvey & Lewis Optical Company. He came in as an apprentice seeking to become an optician so that he could open an optical department in the jewelry store his parents owned in the neighboring town. Joe was a college graduate who was amazed by my experience as a garbage man. On one occasion, I told him I was contemplating selling dinnerware door to door to make extra money. When I mentioned that the dinner plates had a platinum border, Joe corrected me saying that the border was not platinum, but palladium, a member of the platinum family. Joe always rattled off complicated information. He said there are six members of the platinum family: platinum, palladium, osmium, rhodium, ruthenium, and iridium. I told Joe we had to get back to grinding lenses and not talk about dinnerware.

A week later the subject came up again. I told him that I had accepted a job selling dinnerware. As we spoke, I repeated the members of the platinum family to him. He was frozen in place with his mouth wide open. "Did you look that up?" he said slowly.

"No," I repeated, "that's what you told me." He sat on the edge of the bench and said I was wasting my time trying to get an optical license. He said that I should be going to college, that I had the mind for it and that I could drastically improve my life with a college education.

A similar event occurred with Stanley Newcomb, an official at the United Illuminating Company in Connecticut. We met at a gun store where I was buying equipment to load ammunition. Overhearing my conversation, he understood that as an amateur dealing with high explosives, I was in danger. Dressed in a black coat with a black derby hat, carrying a black umbrella, he looked like an Englishman. He said, "I must apologize for having overheard your conversation about the equipment you are purchasing, and I think you stand a very good chance of blowing your head off." I confessed my ignorance about the equipment I was buying. He then took charge and ordered the appropriate equipment I needed and said he would teach me how to reload ammunition safely. He invited me to his home where

I met his wife and three daughters and soon became a member of their family.

Stan had been a pre-med student when he joined the U.S. Navy as a pilot in World War II. He flew a Corsair in the South Pacific and had seen combat. Stan was an erudite scholar who used words seldom heard in general conversation. As usual, he frequently revisited subjects discussed in our conversations weeks earlier. He constantly lost his composure when I repeated the medical terms used to describe illnesses in horses, dogs, and waterfowl. He would drop whatever he held in his hand and remark, "How in God's name do you remember that? You didn't write it down. There's no place you could have heard that except from me weeks ago. These are terms used only in veterinary medicine. You have no idea how intelligent you are. You have much to contribute and you need to finish high school and go to college." I was flattered but never took his advice seriously.

During one of our get-togethers, Stan confided in me that at age forty-seven he decided to leave his prestigious position as a senior vice president at the United Illuminating Company to return to school to study veterinary medicine. The entire community was shocked. He was approaching fifty and felt he could wait no longer to resume his lifelong dream. Little did I know that one day I would follow his example and leave my optical career to attend college as a fulltime student.

ENTER EVELYN CASEY

During the second year of the optical apprenticeship, my wife and I wanted to buy a house but could not get a mortgage because my take-home pay was less than $40 a week. Eager to make more money, I answered an ad in the New Haven paper that said I could earn $50 a week part time in door-to-door sales. I was intrigued by the statuesque gray-haired lady named Evelyn Casey who came to our apartment in response to my inquiry about the ad. I volunteered that I was not smart and that most people believed I was stupid, but that I would like to hear about the job. Undaunted by my comments, she talked for two hours about dinnerware, silver, and crystal. Then she asked if I would like to try the job. I told her that I definitely needed the extra money and wanted the job. I asked how soon I could start? She said that I would first have to become familiar with all of the products we had discussed. I asked what that meant. She said that I would have to learn everything she just told me about the products to make a presentation. I said I was ready. She smiled and said, "You mean you can repeat everything that I just told you?" To her amazement, I went through her entire presentation. Her face showed shock when she said, "You didn't take any notes. I would not believe it if I had not seen it myself. You are not stupid." She told me she taught English at the University of Bridgeport, and added she was confident that with my memory I would have no trouble performing at the university level, adding that she had never seen anything like what I had just demonstrated.

After the presentation, Miss Casey asked why I thought I was stupid. She noted that my spoken grammar was perfect, my vocabulary was extensive, and my use of words was impressive. I told her I learned English from listening to radio programs and watching movies with my mother. I took the job selling dinnerware, crystal, and silverware to prospective brides we found in the society pages where engagements were announced. I was very successful in earning as much money selling dinnerware at night as I made during the week as an apprentice optician. Although I didn't know it at the time, Evelyn Casey was to become one of the most important people in my life. She saw me through a painful divorce and helped me set aside my optical career to enter college as a fulltime student.

Between attending high school at night, and selling dinnerware on weekends, I became a workaholic and neglected my marriage. My marriage originally brought stability to my life, but over the next three years it was not to last. There were issues we could not resolve. We ended in divorce. Being Italian Catholic, our divorce was a major blow to our families. Worst still, for me, it looked like Crazy Mikey was at it again. That was fifty-five years ago, but I still owe Emily, my ex-wife, an enormous debt of gratitude for helping me to become a responsible person. Without her it would never have happened. She controlled all spending; she took my paycheck every week. She determined which bills would be paid and in what order. Gone were the days of my buying fancy clothes, guns, guitars, and expensive dinners. We sacrificed and, within three years, all of my debts were paid, and we had saved $1,400. We borrowed some money from my parents and bought a small house in a suburban neighborhood for $11,900. On the surface, everything was going well, but my commitment to studying optics, selling door to door at night, and playing in a band on weekends put an enormous strain on our marriage, which led to divorce.

Immediately following the divorce, I moved to Norwalk, forty miles from New Haven and took a position as assistant manager of an optical company. Later I moved to Darien where I became the branch manager of Hitchcock and Munson Optical Company. My life had completely changed. I was a highly paid, respected professional, and began a new life.

COLLEGE: A NEW BEGINNING

All during this time, I kept close contact with Evelyn Casey. She continually told me I should get a college education. She encouraged me to take one course at the University of Bridgeport where she taught. I decided to take an evening course in ancient history. I was nervous because I thought I would be exposing my ignorance. The class was mixed with both day students and adults taking the course for college credit. I loved the subject and received an A in the course.

I then took a course in psychology. The instructor was a man named Gerald Winter. My ability to memorize the terms used in psychology and correctly use them in the class intrigued Mr. Winter. He was the first person to notice that I mixed up letters in words and words in a sentence. As a psychologist, Winter quickly grasped two things: 1) I was a learning disabled person, and 2) I had the ability to memorize his lectures. He asked why I was not enrolled as a fulltime student at the university. I told him that to do so I would have to pass the entrance exam at the university, and I could not take multiple-choice tests. He noted that multiple-choice tests were speed and power exams in which I would not necessarily do well. However, he said that my performance at the university was thus far straight A's and that I should consider applying to the university using my performance as the indicator of my capability. I brushed off his suggestion as an impossible task for me. Moreover, to attend school fulltime I would have to abandon my optical career to attend the university. That would erase my career goal of owning my own optical company.

One afternoon, I met with Evelyn Casey who introduced me to the Dean of Students, Dr. Alfred Wolff, a delightful man who told me I was building an excellent reputation at the university. He asked if I was interested in becoming a fulltime student. I told him about my conversation with Gerald Winter, who understood I would never be able to pass an entrance exam based on multiple choice questions. He told me he had spoken to Mr. Winter who agreed with Miss Casey that I should attend University of Bridgeport as a fulltime student. I reiterated to Dr. Wolff that I could not pass the entrance exam because I could not take multiple-choice tests. He smiled and said, "Why would I ask a straight-A student to take an entrance exam? As dean I would simply waive the exam." He said if I entered the university as a fulltime student for one semester and performed at the level I currently performed, he would nominate me for a Dana Scholarship, which would pay my full tuition. "But let us be clear," he said. "This is a scholarship based on performance. You must maintain a top scholar performance to keep the scholarship and also be involved in civic activity at the university." He was convinced that I could do the work.

I thought about it for weeks. I was recently divorced. I could live my life the way I wanted. I wanted to study history, but it meant abandoning my optical career and everything I had been working toward for years. What would my parents think if they saw me abandon my optical career? They might think "Crazy Mikey" was at it again. I decided to pass up the offer. Dr. Wolff was not offended because he knew that my leaving my optical career would be a tremendous decision. But he remained a close friend, calling me occasionally to congratulate me on my continued performance.

Another semester passed. Again, I received straight A's. Dr. Wolff met with me and told me the faculty really wanted me to be a fulltime student. He was prepared to offer me an academic scholarship and again said that I had to be a fulltime student at least for one semester before I would be eligible. I agonized over the offer as I was now managing the branch office of an optical company, and at that time was making very good money. It was clear that after working so hard to obtain the status I enjoyed, I would have to give it up and return to the bottom of a different ladder without an income. I went to Charlie Hitchcock, the owner of the optical company whose partner had recently died. I told Charlie that I decided to attend the university fulltime. Charlie then raised the ante. He offered me a partnership in the firm to take the place of his deceased partner. He said he would sign an agreement with me to give me forty percent equity in the company and that he would then transfer the rest of the company to me over the next ten years. My head was spinning. This was a dream opportunity. It meant financial security and the prestige of being a business owner.

But I was genuinely excited about attending the university. I told Charlie that if I took his offer, I would be working five and a half days a week making eyeglasses for people who were traveling all over the world and seeing the world through my glasses, and I would be sitting in that store for the rest of my life. He was disappointed at first. I watched his shoulders drop and a wave of uncertainty cross his face. Then he said he always wanted to be in the newspaper business and that he took a job as an optical apprentice until he could find a newspaper that would hire him. "That was forty years ago," he said, "and I'm still here making eyeglasses." He then smiled and shook my hand with both of his hands and told me if I ever needed his help, he would always be there for me. I suppressed all of my fears and told Dr. Wolff I would leave the optical profession and enter the university as a fulltime student. That was the second major change in my life. Following Stan Newcomb's example, I left a highly lucrative career to attend the university fulltime.

My mother was supportive, but my father went ballistic. "You left a high-paying job to go to school! What's wrong with you?" he asked. It appeared to everyone that Crazy Mikey had returned.

The challenge of attending college was daunting. While in night high school, I could easily manage my workload because there were only a few subjects to master. In college, my dyslexia was another matter. Unlike night school, where I easily kept pace with one or two courses, in college I was required to take five courses each semester. In my case these included Spanish, astronomy, English literature, and two different history courses. The lectures were no trouble. I did not take notes but simply listened to the instructor. If I had attempted to take notes, I would have lost the instructor's message because I would have been concentrating on spelling the words used in the lecture rather than listening. So, through most of the courses, I never took notes. However, the reading assignments took massive amounts of time. There was no shortcut. I simply had to focus on the words and repeat passages out loud where I detected words that I would see in reverse order or did not see at all. Words like "always," "never," "not," etc.; words that totally changed the meaning of the passage if misread. Or, I might misread a descriptive word that was the essence of the sentence. For me, reading each paragraph more than once was required. Although this reading problem was a major handicap both in high school and in college, no one ever noticed that handicap. Why would they? I generally got an A in the courses. They never saw what went on behind closed doors when I was studying.

I had experienced all of these visual problems previously, but I never connected them with a learning disability. I never heard the term dyslexia until well after I left graduate school. I assumed that my poor performance before I quit high school was an indication that I was intellectually inferior to everyone else. My disability was hidden from everyone, including me. It took years of becoming a top scholar in both undergraduate and graduate studies to slowly convince myself I was not inferior to my classmates.

During that first semester of being back in school fulltime, I was terrified of failure. Oh, sure, I had done well, but that was only as a part-time student. Plus, I had my job to fall back on. But, as a fulltime student, I would be up against serious competition; the students would be smarter in the day classes as opposed to the night classes where I had done well. What if I flunked out? There was a promise of a scholarship, but I had to maintain my grade-point average to obtain that scholarship. If I failed, there would be no place to hide. My friends and family would say, there goes Crazy Mikey again. He quit a good job and then flunked out of college.

As it turned out, all of that anxiety was for nothing. At the end of that first semester, I earned a straight "A" average and was contacted by Dr. Wolff, who came through with a full Dana Scholarship. I was off and running. As a fulltime student I participated in many school activities and was a member of an academic honor society.

Of special note was a course I took in astronomy from Professor Philip Stern, who also lectured at the Hayden Planetarium in New York and was setting up a planetarium in Bridgeport. I was fascinated by his lectures. They were explosive. Mr. Stern, like all of my other professors, was intrigued by my ability to repeat his lectures verbatim. After I passed his course, he asked me to lead his class while he was out of town. Then he asked me to do the Christmas show at the planetarium. I was frightened to death, but I did it. Suddenly, I was a regular at the Bridgeport Planetarium presenting public lectures on the stars that appeared in the different seasons. The local radio stations always covered my public appearances, which was incredible to me considering how many hours I spent listening to the radio when I was growing up. My work at the planetarium was the talk of the university.

As I approached graduation, several professors urged me to go on to graduate school. I had honestly not thought about it. My undergraduate degree was in history; to be a history teacher, they said, I would need at least a master's degree. I even considered law school, but I was fearful of taking the law boards because, like all qualifying exams they, too, were multiple choice.

One of my professors, Dr. Dison Poe, who taught Oriental philosophy at Bridgeport, suggested that I shift majors in graduate school to study political theory. Dr. Poe was a visiting professor who had been Minister of Education for Nationalist China before the communist revolution. I had taken a few courses with him and relied on his global experience to advise me. He argued that I should apply to the University of Chicago, Stanford in California, and Georgetown in Washington, DC. Of course, I would still have to take the Graduate Record Exam (GRE), which is supposed to demonstrate what you have learned as an undergraduate student and determine your suitability for graduate studies. To do so I would be facing another multiple-choice obstacle. I took the exam and performed as anticipated. My faculty advisor said my performance was dismal. But psychology professor Gerald Winter reminded me that multiple-choice exams do not predict an individual's success and that I should apply to all of the schools Dr. Poe suggested. Both Mr. Winter and Dr. Poe believed I should apply to Ivy League schools. They recommended the University of Chicago, Stanford University, and Georgetown University.

A CALL FROM GEORGETOWN UNIVERSITY

I was almost immediately rejected by Stanford University and the University of Chicago. Then, one night early in the spring at about 9:30 pm, I received a phone call from a soft-spoken man. He asked how it was that a *magna cum laude* graduate could do so poorly on the GRE's. Without asking his name, I told him about my inability to take multiple-choice tests, and that I studied under the toughest professors who always gave essay exams. He responded that he also had trouble with multiple-choice tests and that no one at the Graduate School in Georgetown used multiple-choice exams.

I asked to whom I was speaking. He responded, "I'm Father James B. Horrigan, S.J., Dean of the Graduate School at Georgetown."

I asked why he was calling me at 9:30 at night. He laughed saying he was a Jesuit priest, "What else am I going to do at night?" He said the admissions faculty at Georgetown were intrigued with my background and my undergraduate performance, and that he was authorized to offer me a fellowship to study political theory at Georgetown. He added that the terms of the fellowship required me to enter a PhD program and bypass the master's degree. The scholarship offered a monthly stipend and other benefits. However, the offer required me to begin a summer program in June immediately after my graduation from Bridgeport.

I accepted Father Horrigan's offer and went to Washington to meet with him. I arrived in Washington during a freak snowstorm that closed the entire city. Abandoning my car in a snowdrift on M Street, I walked uphill to the Georgetown campus. When I slipped and began to fall, I was caught by a young graduate student walking behind me. His name was Jose Sorzano. He and his family were Cuban refugees. When he heard my reason for being in Washington and that I had abandoned my car and had no hotel reservation, he insisted that I stay at his home. We were marooned for at least four days. We talked until the city and the school reopened days later. During that time, I expressed all of my fears about not being able to perform at Georgetown. He assured me that I would succeed. He helped me select the courses I should take and the professors who taught them. We became best friends. We studied for our comprehensives over the next three years, and both received our degrees with distinction. From that fateful snow day forward, Jose and I began a friendship that has lasted nearly sixty years.

When the snow melted, I finally met with Father Horrigan, who introduced me to Dr. Karl Cerny, the Chairman of the Government Department. Cerny explained that several faculty members were interested in my personal history and academic record, but most were out for the summer. Instead, he recommended that, during the summer, I work with a young instructor named Jeane Kirkpatrick. She was still working on her PhD and asked to be assigned as my advisor. We met at Jeane's home where we talked over the sound of three young rambunctious boys, an overweight Labrador retriever named Linda who barked loudly, and a deaf cat named Phillip. Again, unbeknownst to me at the time, like Evelyn Casey, Jeane Kirkpatrick was to become a major force in my life.

Jeane noted that I had not taken a single course in political science as an undergraduate, let alone in political theory. Knowing my deficiencies in political theory, she listed books that I was to read and discuss with her weekly. She took me through the classics and the modern era of theory. She also picked professors whose courses I should take. Both Jeane and her husband took an interest in me. I attended dinners with guests at their home. Many of the guests were major figures in the Democratic Party, academicians, columnists, and journalists. It was through Jeane that I met Senator Hubert Humphrey who later ran for President against Richard Nixon in 1968. Jeane and I spent hours each week during my four years of coursework and two years during the writing of my dissertation. Sixteen years later, Jeane Kirkpatrick became the U.S. Ambassador to the United Nations and Jose Sorzano became her Deputy. Jeane mentored my dissertation and, until her death, she was my advisor and a close personal friend.

I mention all of the people cited in this section, because they were key to my ability to travel the road from garbage collector to PhD. They invested their time to help me as they did others. I was fortunate to find them and trusted their judgment. All of these people had faith in me and motivated me to take on new challenges. My good fortune continued when, in 1968, I met Denise Wiens, a young graduate student in her first year at Georgetown. I was preparing for my doctoral comprehensives; she was beginning a master's program. Jeane became a close friend to both of us and was pleased when we decided to marry. Jeane, along with other members of my Georgetown faculty, had become my family. Denise and I were married in 1971 at the home of the Sorzanos with family, friends and my faculty members in attendance.

Presidential Recognition

Following the award of my doctorate, Georgetown University notified the local press of the unusual nature of my candidacy. On June 9, 1971, the Evening Star carried a front-page story titled "Garbage Man to PhD" that focused on my background as a former high-school dropout and garbage collector.[4] The story centered on my working-class background as well as my knowledge and understanding of immigrant communities. The article also focused on my belief in the achievement ethic and my fear that it was under attack. Most importantly, I cited President Nixon as an exponent of the achievement ethic and envisioned him as a president who could restore America's faith in that traditional value. Shortly after the article appeared, I was contacted by Jerry Jones of the White House Personnel Office and was appointed to the White House staff as Special Assistant to the President. Suddenly, articles on my White House activities began to appear in the national press. There was a front-page story in *The Wall Street Journal* about my working-class background that included my background as a high-school dropout who was fired from scores of jobs and my history as a garbage collector. There were similar articles in major newspapers in other cities. Then there were two articles in *Life* magazine that covered my activities in the White House. All of these stories appeared in the president's morning news summary. It was clear that I had become a spokesman for the president and the work ethic.

In 1973, President Nixon appointed me to direct ACTION, the newly created federal agency overseeing America's volunteer programs. I directed the domestic anti-poverty social programs and the international Peace Corps. Later, in 1977, I joined the American Enterprise Institute as a visiting scholar where I wrote monographs about my government experience and worked on a special project dealing with American labor unions. While at AEI, I widened my circle of contacts, not only in the labor movement, but in corporate America. In 1985, I established my own company, Balzano Associates, which offers advice to corporate CEOs seeking to establish a closer relationship with their workforce.

In my experience, the key to success in America is commitment, hard work, and adherence to the work ethic. I had a great advantage in that I was surrounded with teachers and an entire community who taught me that success or failure was largely in my own hands, I just had to roll up my sleeves and dig in. I was also open to the possibility of growing as a person by meeting new friends, especially friends who were smarter than I was.

In chapter one of this book, I referred to Tommy, the young boy I met when we both repeated third grade. We remained friends all of our lives. Tommy was a good boy—he never played hooky with me, but we did roam the docks together. Following my divorce and college career, he, along with three other friends, remained in my close circle of friends. One night at dinner his wife cautiously asked me a question that is relevant to this book. "Mikey," she said, "you were always hanging on street corners with all the other guys and doing crazy things, then you disappeared for years, and all of a sudden you were in the White House advising the President. How did that happen?"

My answer to her is relevant to every high-school dropout, current and future, as well as their families and academic influencers who may read this book. We are all equally born stupid. What makes us different are the people we meet during our lifetime. I was blessed by finding people who knew more than I did and by knowing to follow their example. Every contact I made opened new contacts with newer and even smarter people. If you stay in the same neighborhood all your life, you are limited by the friends you meet on those neighborhood blocks. Branching out can be somewhat risky, but it enables you to break the circle that surrounds you. The more people you meet, the more likely your behavior will be subject to change for the better.

In this chapter, I have tried to focus on the positive influence of adults I encountered who encouraged me to improve myself. They did so first by recognizing that I had talent that had not been recognized during the first 20 years of my life. I recommend to parents that they should encourage their children to meet adults outside their normal social groups. In my case, they unquestionably were the reason for my success. Ironically, none of these people identified me as learning disabled, but then neither did my parents, teachers, guidance counselors or military officers. What they did do was believe in me.

LEARNING DISABILITIES
AND THE FEAR OF FAILURE

Whether returning to high school to get a GED, entering a management training program, going into the military, or starting an apprenticeship in any of the crafts, anyone will encounter a fear of failure. I experienced fear of failure throughout the time when I was learning a trade and attending high school. I found that being an F student at the bottom of the class was a safe place for me. I believed I was stupid, so I did not try to improve myself. Being considered stupid protected me from criticism or being laughed at if I failed. Only when you are engaged in an effort to improve yourself do you run the risk of failure and ridicule. In my case, I avoided the risks by not trying and by living up to the failure label I was given.

I was afraid to take the job at the American Optical Company when Ray offered it to me. I believed that I would fail to perform and would be let go within the first few days of starting the job, as I had with all of the other jobs that I had lost or quit. Even though I expected to fail, I decided to try anyway, but I still expected to fail. To my surprise, day after day I succeeded in performing those tasks to which I was assigned. Days turned to weeks, weeks into months, months into years, as I constantly improved.

After working hours, Ray and a few other apprentices met at night to study optical theory. At first, I was afraid to admit that while I could perform the manual operations required on the job, optical theory was another story. Optical theory consisted of understanding diagrams and definitions, and a theory of how light passes through a lens. I quickly memorized the definitions and compared them to the lenses shown in the photos. Suddenly, the theory was understandable. Step by step I overcame my fears and increased my confidence.

When I returned to high school for my GED, it was a new experience. Before I dropped out of high school as a teenager, I had no fear of failure. I expected to fail. Now, officials at the American Optical Company were expecting me to succeed. I was once again gripped with a fear of failure. Classes were held at night. Most of the attendees were adults who had also quit school. I formed a friendship with an older man from Pittsburg Plate Glass Company whose employer said they would promote him if he obtained a high-school diploma. We entered the classes together: American History, English, Literature and Ancient History.

Unlike in my childhood, I read the homework assignments with great interest. Admittedly, I was slow. I noticed that I had to read each passage several times. The words still flipped around in the sentences. So, I read them out loud to hear and make sense of them. In class, the teachers repeated what was in the homework assignment. I understood everything that was said. When teachers engaged students during the lectures, I responded with the right answer every time. Others either remained quiet or responded incorrectly. It was clear to me that I was not dumb. I did not know if the others were not smart, but on oral questions in class or written tests, I passed with ease while many of them did not. Like the optical theory I had studied earlier, I found the assignments understandable and enjoyable.

Even with all of that, graduating from high school did not remove my fear of failure when I started night classes in college. Initially I was fearful, because college was not high school. I took courses as a non-matriculated student. That is, I was not receiving college credit for the course because I was not enrolled at the college. I knew that if I received a low grade it did not count unless I enrolled in the college seeking a degree. The instructors used the same techniques as did the high school teachers. We were given reading assignments. There were lectures. I had the same problem with reading that I had in high school, so I applied the same techniques. I read aloud and passed all the exams with ease.

As in high school, the instructors engaged the classes in Q&A. Again, I always seemed to know the answer the instructors wanted. When they called on students around the room, only a few could answer the questions. This did not mean that I concluded I was smart, but rather that the night students were not as smart as those who attended school during the day. When I agreed to attend the University of Bridgeport on a fulltime basis, I was terrified. The classes were filled with fulltime students who had passed the college entrance exams that I could not pass. But once in the classroom, my fears evaporated. Students came unprepared for class participation and had either not read the assignments or did not understand them. My fear of failure drove me to prepare thoroughly, enabling me to perform at my best.

As I entered my junior and senior years, the fear had lessened. By this point, I had dedicated my life to my studies. Many students had come to college as though they were going to Disneyland. They had a ball. However, my personal enjoyment was in the classes. I loved every minute of my undergraduate study.

When I entered Georgetown University, the same fears resurfaced. Wow! This was a PhD program, after all. All of the students were the best of the best in their undergraduate colleges, many of them from Ivy League schools. At Georgetown, students were challenged to read, think, and create. Most of my professors gave lectures that were fascinating and sought interaction with class participants. Preparing thoroughly was my solution to overcoming my fear of failure.

All during these years I developed techniques to help work around my dyslexia. On some occasions I would read sections of the assigned reading into a tape recorder and listen to the lectures. This avoided the flipping of words in the paragraphs. I created lectures of my own that I gave to family and friends. I discovered that, for me, the best way to understand a subject was to teach it to someone else. Then I could pick out the essential elements in the subject.

I also made lists of obvious questions that I expected instructors to ask on exams. These included what I call "what did I tell you in class" questions. Professors expect students to master major points made during lectures: there are three reasons for this and four reasons for that, etc. The night before a test I would lock myself in the building where the test would be given the next morning. I wrote my answers to expected questions on the chalkboards around the room. Three of these. Four of these, etc. I would rehearse the anticipated questions and the answers by looking at the boards. Before sunrise, I would erase the boards so there was no trace of chalk on them. Then I went home, got a few hours of sleep, returned to that same room for the exam, and used the mental recall of those items I had written on each board.

Fear is a constant companion for anyone seeking to return to school, especially if you were a poor student before dropping out. During my entire educational career, I had to deal with this emotion. But I can assure you, as my fears were totally unfounded, so are yours. If you think about it, your performance in high school might have been poor because you either did not care about your grades or would not try. What happens in middle school is that you get into a rut of past low or failing grades that creates momentum toward failure. Even when at times you try to reverse the downward trend, the momentum of direction is almost impossible to overcome because to turn your grades from D to C requires going back to earlier stages of coursework you did not master. It's like coming into a movie in the middle. You have to go back to the beginning. And you can. In fact, your memory will help you more than you think. I found it easier to get good grades the second time around because I applied myself. That's my number one tip for anyone in the same situation: apply yourself. You are as smart as anyone else in your class. You can make it. You can turn your life around.

Success does not mean you will be free from self-doubts. Everyone in life has a self-conscious fear of failure. Moreover, repeated success does not eliminate this ingrained fear. When I was in my fifties and had a record as an advisor to several U.S.

presidents and was running a thriving business, I was frustrated by how long it took me to read a page, a report or a news article. I envied close friends of mine who could read a page as fast as they could turn it and could repeat the content when they finished. I decided to take one of the many rapid reading courses advertised on a local radio station. I entered an evening program held at a Holiday Inn in Arlington, Virginia. It was like night school all over again. The room was filled with adults seeking to improve their reading speed. We were instructed to move our hand across a page from top to bottom and glance, not read, the passages as our hand passed over the page. The rest of the class did quite well. But because of my dyslexia, the words that normally shifted in a sentence continued to shift but they did so at a faster rate, requiring me to reread the sentence until it made sense. Suddenly all of my fears of inadequacy resurfaced. It was like middle school all over again. I was at the bottom of the class. Faced with embarrassment and fear, I ran away from that program.

I confessed all of this to my wife when she asked why I was no longer attending the reading class. Knowing me as well as she does, she put this experience in the context of my history. My dyslexia was overriding the motion of my hand moving over the page. The words were still displaced. I remembered what Professor Gerald Winter said, that rapid reading was not an indicator of my intelligence or my ability to succeed in life or to master complex theories. It only meant I would not be able to read at high speed or perform well on multiple-choice tests.

It is important for parents who read this book to know that I am as dyslexic now as I was when I was a child. Being dyslexic made studying difficult, but it did not prevent me from becoming a top scholar in two universities and a successful businessman, and it will not prevent your child from succeeding in their chosen path as well. I have said all of this because you may have a child who will be fearful of continuing or going back to school. It's important to be patient and supportive, and to help them develop strategies for the learning challenges they face. Remember, they must want to succeed. You can help them by listening to their desires and encouraging them to engage in what's interesting to them, even if it means overcoming obstacles. I did it, and so can they.

Kindergarten, 1940, with
Sister Morris DeLorita.
My mother always dressed
me in all white.

My father, Michael
Balzano, escorting me
into my first grade class
from kindergarten.

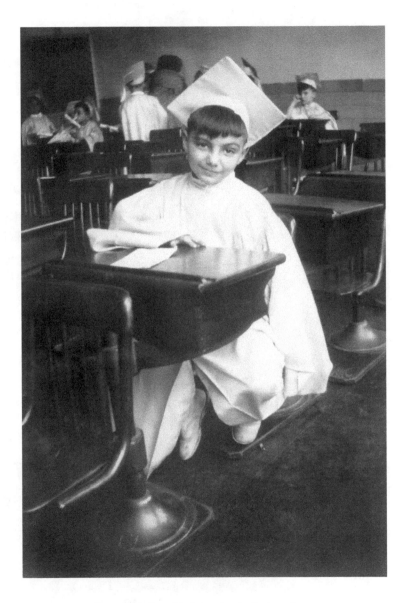

Promotion from kindergarten to first grade.

Sunday outfit: after church in our back yard. 8 years old.

My mother's sister, Aunt Mary, and her boyfriend.

My mother, Jennie Balzano, and me.

The gang in New York City: when we left Yankee Stadium to go to Times Square.

Tommy Scelzo, life-long friend, and me at East Haven Beach.

Frank D'Amato, my guitar
teacher and counselor.

My headshot for a
professional guitar job.

My brother Anthony, whose stage name was Tony Zane,

"Harmonica Virtuoso."

My brother Anthony, "Harmonic Virtuoso," (foreground) and me (back left), playing at a wedding.

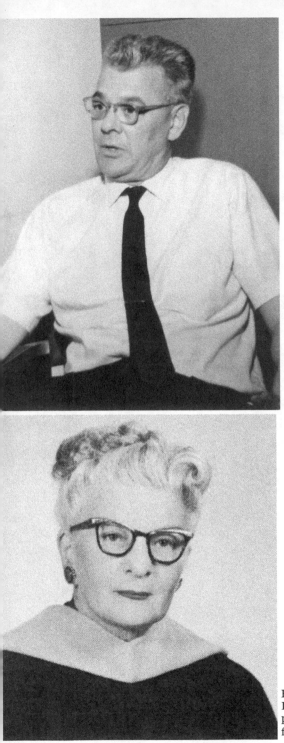

Stanley Newcomb, a key advisor
in my life, corporate executive, and
later Doctor of Veterinary Medicine.

Evelyn Casey, University English
Instructor, the person who made it
possible for me to enter university
fulltime.

Joe Pasqualini (center), Ray Boffa (right) and me at the American Optical Compa

Michael Balzano, optician, in front of optical shop, New Hav

My wife Denise and me in the Oval Office at my swearing-in ceremony to be Director of the ACTION Agency, 1973. District Court Judge Nunzio (second from right) and President Richard Nixon.

PART II
Hope for Others

Chapter 4

For Parents

In the introduction and first part of this book, I offered my life story with the hope that it could be useful to parents with learning disabled children or children engaged in antisocial behavior. As one who speaks in public, I have discovered that my experience offers hope to parents struggling to help children exhibiting behavior problems similar to those I exhibited in my childhood. I often hear, "If you could do it, maybe my child can do it, too."

When asked for advice, I always begin by stating that I am not a clinician. I have not studied control groups of problem children to formulate strategies for dealing with behavior problems. The experiences shared in this book recount the chapters of my life as a troubled youth who began a journey from being called "Crazy Mikey" to one who now enjoys more than his fair share of influence both in industry and the national public policy arena.

What I do tell parents, however, is that their children's situation is not hopeless. Their children can be productive members of society and lead satisfying lives. Their child's future will depend on emotional support and love. Looking back on my childhood, it is clear that I had both.

As I have described, my dyslexia went undetected while I was in school. It certainly was never understood by my parents, who had very little formal education themselves. Moreover, as working-class immigrants struggling to survive, they lacked both the time and the sophistication to deal with a learning disability. My lack of interest in school was normal for many children in my community. The ability for young people to be employed in the factories that required only manual labor could have masked the learning disabilities of many of the neighborhood children. These young people simply disappeared into the factories.

It should also be remembered that dyslexia was not widely recognized in the thirties and forties when I was in school. It is likely that neither the nuns, excellent teachers though they were, nor the public school teachers were aware of the existence of such a condition. Even today the problem is often unrecognized, overlooked or ignored.

When dealing with inner city schools where parents are likely to be in the same socio-economic strata as my parents, I suspect they, too, might lack the sophistication to detect a learning disability that might explain their child's poor academic performance or antisocial behavior. If the teachers do not detect it, there is little chance that either the student's low academic achievement or antisocial behavior will be corrected.

PARENTS WITH YOUNG CHILDREN

Most of the parents who approach me fall into two categories: parents with very young children in the lower grades, and those with teenagers in middle and high school. In the first category, many of these parents feel hopeless because they have no experience in detecting, let alone treating, learning disorders. These parents expect the school system to identify and treat these disorders. But this is rarely the case. When parents in this category approach me, they appear to be desperate and at a loss for solutions. Three examples are instructive.

While attending a conference at the Broadmoor Hotel in Colorado Springs three years ago, I was in a photo reception line to meet the keynote speaker. I was carrying a copy of a book that I had recently published and wanted to give him. Knowing that it would be inappropriate to hand it to him in that environment, I decided to wait until all the photo ops were finished. But I did mention the book to him during our photo and told him I would get it to him before the conference ended. I moved to a corner of the room where a group of hotel staff were assembled watching the event. A few were dressed in hotel jackets, clearly identifying them as the ever-present hotel staff eager to assist guests.

As I stood there, with the book in my hand, a lovely lady who was not wearing a hotel jacket approached me with a big smile on her face; she asked if I needed assistance. She said her name was Ann Alba. I later learned that she manages the entire 784-room hotel and conference center. When I told her of my intention to give my book to the speaker, she offered to get the book to him. I handed her the book and noticed that she focused on the back cover that states that I was a high school dropout. She asked why I had dropped out of school. I told her that I was undiagnosed as learning disabled as a child. As I spoke, the smile on her face disappeared to form a laser-like stare. Before I could ask her if I had said something offensive, she took me by the hand and led me several feet to another young woman also without a hotel uniform. This woman, too, wore a broad smile on her face, eager to assist me. Ann introduced me to the second woman whose name is Shauna S. Ann told Shauna that I was Dr. Balzano who was once a learning disabled child. The smile on Shauna's face suddenly disappeared and changed to a cold stare. Tears flooded her eyes and ran down her cheeks. I thought, *what did I say to offend these women?* Shauna said her son had been identified as learning disabled and that the school said there was nothing they could do to help him. She said she was beside herself worrying there would be no hope he could live a normal life. As it turned out she had never confided that information about his condition to anyone except Ann. "Since you are a doctor," she said, "then you have managed to overcome your disabilities. That means that there is hope my Jack can live a normal life." That was the beginning of a long series of conversations.

She said the school system offered no help for his condition so the family moved to a higher income area in the city thinking the new school system would focus on their child's disability. But, like the former school, teachers and administrators in the new school refused to acknowledge or recognize the term dyslexia because they did not have the money to treat it. I told her that she was going to have to go beyond teachers in the school to the administrator and insist on special treatment for her child.

The most important thing was for her to believe her child would make it. I said every child has natural abilities that can offset their particular learning disorder, and that it was up to her, and to each of Jack's teachers, to find his natural gifts and help him develop them. I explained that in my case, my gift was an ability to memorize conversations and lectures, but that did not mean I could perform well on multiple-choice tests. I further explained that I eventually developed ways of compensating for those problems and stated that, with her help and patience, so would Jack. I told her that some of the world's greatest achievers were dyslexic (Albert Einstein and Walt Disney, for instance) and their learning disabilities did not prevent them from becoming successful. As we talked, I could see my comments were reassuring her that her son could be successful despite his dyslexia.

Following the conference, Shauna and I spoke many times about the problems I had as a child that were compounded by the fact that no one in the school system recognized I had a learning disability called "dyslexia." I was a PhD with honors in my mid-40s before I ever heard the term. I told her that I have achieved academic, economic, and social success despite my disabilities, and so could Jack. I pointed out that her child had a major advantage in that his parents recognized the problem and were committed to helping him. That was the beginning of a friendship with her family.

Checking on Jack recently, I learned he has a new teacher who is well aware of his challenges and is working with him to overcome them. The good thing is that everyone is aware of Jack's situation, hence, there is little chance that he will develop internal conflicts or antisocial behavior in frustration. Again, it is important for the parents I counsel to understand that I never outgrew my dyslexia, but in the end, it did not hinder my success. I made it in life in spite of my disabilities, and so can their children.

One year later at the same conference, I was approached by a young woman who asked if I was the person who had helped Shauna with her dyslexic child. She said she knew of a conference participant, Marie G., who wanted to speak with me. Marie and her husband are professionals who had been struggling with the school systems in Colorado and

Michigan that would not identify their son Max as dyslexic but rather as a child who was disruptive and not ready for school. It was at this time when Marie and her husband decided to go outside of the school system. Over the past year and a half, she saw her son losing ground while attending public school in Michigan. Max, who loved to listen to her read stories to him, slowly became disinterested.

As she spoke, I could not help but recall that I, too, enjoyed having someone read to me. In fact, when teachers in my classes in grade school read history or poetry aloud, I stopped clowning around. I was actually learning by listening to the teacher. I have never outgrown this tendency. I have had people read aloud the articles, op-ed pieces and drafts of everything I have written, including the draft of this very book.

Marie and her husband brought all of their observations about Max to the attention of his teacher who had no explanation as to why Max appeared to be losing ground. She brought her case to the school administrators. Again, no explanation, but clearly the inference was that Max might have unspecified learning disabilities. Fearing that Max could be labeled as a severely troubled youth, perhaps even retarded, the parents removed him from the public school system and began homeschooling.

Over time, they have paid for a variety of tests, none of which identified their son as severely disturbed. In fact, homeschooling has had a definite impact on Max. First, he once again enjoys having stories and lessons read to him, which to me indicates that he learns better by listening than reading. Second, he had demonstrated an interest in science, which was an area of possible strength and motivation. Max has accepted every challenge. When faced with a new one, Max says, "If Mike can do it, I can do it."

Like Shauna's son Jack, Max has the advantage of having two educated parents who are committed to his success. Their love and patience will win out. But it is clear that both sets of parents are on their own. There appear to be few allies in the local or state government to help their or other learning disabled children.

In my experience, parents have responded to their dyslexic children at the grammar school level in different ways. Shauna moved her son Jack to a different school. Marie, fearful that her child could be mistakenly labeled as retarded, chose to remove him from the public school system and began homeschooling.

A third approach was selected by a woman I have known since the 1950s. I met Rae when I was helped by her father, Stanley Newcomb, mentioned earlier in this book. Rae and her husband lived in Underhill, Vermont, where she was a high school and college teacher. When their son Geoff was seven, they were told he was retarded by his first grade teacher. Confident that their son was not retarded, Rae removed him from the school, placed him temporarily in a Montessori pre-school and worked with the staff. Within a month, the child stopped nail biting and acting out and began reading. An extremely well-educated woman, Rae launched into a massive research project to identify learning centers specializing in techniques to address the needs of their child. In Vermont she found the newly created Stern Center for Language and Learning. In addition to tutoring their son, the Center worked with her and the public school to develop and monitor appropriate IEPs (individual education plans) for him through elementary and middle grades. The approach that worked for their son, and is fundamental to the Stern Center, is called the Orton-Gillingham method (see Appendix 3).

At the age of 13, identified as extremely intelligent, their son went to The Landmark School outside of Boston at the suggestion of the Stern Center, and then to West Virginia Wesleyan College where the entire faculty had been trained in the Orton-Gillingham approach. Geoff earned a degree in computer science and developed the confidence he now enjoys as an adult. Today he is a perfectly adjusted young professional in the competitive world of Silicon Valley.

In doing research for this book, I have been constantly surprised by the number of parents I encounter who are currently dealing with, or have dealt with, a child identified as learning disabled. While discussing the requirements for including photos for this book with the consultant, Shannon K., that we have used for years, she became emotionally moved by the stories of the other parents discussed in the book. She then told us of her experience.

When Shannon was faced with the diagnosis that her 5-year old son was learning disabled, she chose to work within the public school system. She credits their success to three factors. First, she found early intervention and support. Second, at each stage of her son's development, she worked with a teacher advocate who could say and do things on her son's behalf which, if demanded by a parent, would likely have caused efforts to fail. Third, she was not a hysterical parent defending her son. She remained calm, credible and engaged which allowed her to marshal resources for her son that otherwise might not have been available. Again, an educated professional, she knew that if she was overcome by emotion she would have been dismissed as a hysterical parent. Because of her efforts to ensure her son received the appropriate educational resources at every level in the public school, today her son is a college graduate.

Although each of the four children described in this chapter exhibited behaviors which indicated a learning disability, at no time did the schools request testing. The implication to the parents was their children were slow learners, perhaps even retarded. But the parents persevered, each taking a slightly different approach. They sought to avoid having their children labeled inappropriately, and all of them devoted enormous amounts of time, financial resources, and suffered emotional strain to ensure success for their children.

But what would be the case for working class parents in less affluent communities, or children in inner city school systems? Would the parents have the time, experience, and finances to recognize and address their children's problems? I suspect that, like my working class family, they would be busy surviving. I was never diagnosed or treated as a child, but simply dismissed as an incorrigible "crazy Mikey."

It is important for parents to understand that children do not outgrow dyslexia, but with appropriate intervention can learn and be successful. I have learned that a benefit of the Orton-Gillingham approach is that parents can apply its methods at home, thereby reinforcing what happens in school to further success for their children.

Dyslexia occurs without regard to family social standing, parental education, or financial means. I fervently believe all children deserve an education appropriate to their needs. That is why I have written this book. There are a lot of Crazy Mikeys whose parents and teachers need the support of professional organizations and learning centers dedicated to diagnosing and teaching learning disabled children. The Appendix in this book can provide some of that support and will no doubt lead to other resources available in local school districts.

I am certain that today's elementary, middle, and high school teachers are well aware of dyslexia and other learning disabilities, but they are not clinicians and although they might detect learning problems, parents should not hold teachers responsible for treating such problems. However, teachers should inform parents of their suspicions and inform the school counselor that they suspect a particular learning disability in a specific student. Teachers and counselors can provide guidance to parents so they can find help for their child. Teachers are there to teach and help as many students as possible, but they cannot be expected to possess the specialized training to correct the learning problems of individual students. Ideally, however, they should be involved in identifying such students and informing the parents.

That said, from my experience, today it is clear that parents of learning disabled children are pretty much on their own with respect to diagnosing the disorder. In many states dyslexia is not even considered a disorder, which means the teachers, whether in inner city, suburban or rural schools, will not be able to help them. It will be up to the parents to find help outside the school system.

But it is worse than that. In a documentary titled *Hard to Read: How American Schools Fail Kids with Dyslexia*, Emily Hanford[5] notes that across the country public schools not only fail to identify children as dyslexic but deny them treatment. Hanford describes case studies where parents suspected their children were dyslexic as early as kindergarten but were told not to worry because their children would improve over time. Many of these parents had their children evaluated outside of the school system and found they were, in fact, dyslexic. When the parents reported the test results to the school system, they were told that the children had learning disabilities but were not dyslexic. When parents asked why the school psychologist refused to use the word dyslexic they were told "it is not in our realm of professionalism to say a child is dyslexic."

Hanford found that public schools nationwide refuse to use the word dyslexic. They do so "to avoid providing special education services required by federal law, services the schools do not have the funds to pursue." Hanford argued that having conducted dozens of interviews with parents, other researchers, lawyers, and teachers across the country, dyslexic students are overwhelmingly ignored.

The National Center for Education Statistics found only 4.5% of public-school students are treated for dyslexia while scientists estimate that between 5-12% percent of all U.S. school children actually have dyslexia.

Dr. Sally Shaywitz of the Yale Center for Dyslexia and Creativity, author of *Overcoming Dyslexia*,[6] argues that dyslexics go unrecognized well beyond their adolescent years. She notes that there are proven ways to treat dyslexia that are not new or even controversial. Still, after parents pay tens of thousands of dollars treating their children, school officials refuse to believe the tests, arguing that they do not agree with the test results. Most parents interviewed in the Hanford report had to pay for services themselves that amounted to thousands of dollars.

And yet the Department of Education has issued directives requiring school systems to use the word dyslexia, which the school systems refuse to use. Federal law requires that dyslexic children be treated, but the schools refuse to do so. In a family of five dyslexic children in Baltimore, Maryland, the parents retained an attorney and spent $350,000 to argue their case that federal law was being ignored. That family succeeded in getting their five children into a "lab school for children with learning disabilities."[7]

From my conversations with such parents, it is clear that many do not know where to turn. Ironically, when I talk to parents with dyslexic children, they express hope that if I overcame my learning disabilities and became successful, then their children could do so as well. To be clear, I am as dyslexic today as I was in kindergarten. I never overcame that learning disability. My behavior problems were partially the result of my learning disabilities. It took the help of friends and personal self-determination to overcome my antisocial behavior. While I was successful in doing that, I was unsuccessful in reversing my dyslexia.

I attribute my success in life to my entering an optical apprenticeship. The apprenticeship required discipline I did not have while in school. It taught me discipline. That is why I offer the suggestion that students consider initially pursuing other options than going directly to college from high school. That does not mean that they will not go to college later in life. They could do so after they acquire the skills and the discipline to complete the apprenticeship, as I did. For me, it was a necessary step in the process. Many parents believe that success in life requires a college education. It was not so in my case. The college education came after I became a craftsman.

TEACHERS ALWAYS HAVE AN IMPACT

My sympathy goes out to those teachers who are trying to educate troublemakers like I was as a child. When I was not laughing and joking, I sat in the back of the room and appeared like a corpse. But, no one knew that I was listening to the various lectures given by my teachers. The reason I was so quiet was because I was enjoying the lectures and I was learning—the poetry they read aloud, and the history of the Greeks and Romans. I remember all of my teachers and the subjects they taught. The problem was I could not do the reading, arithmetic or pass a written test. If any of my teachers would have asked me a question on what they told the class, I could have answered any of their questions.

The daughter of one of my corporate clients was teaching in an inner-city school. She shared with her father the frustration she experienced with students who sounded a lot like me. I asked him if I could write to her. He looked at me askance and asked me to give him the letter for review before he passed it on to her. Although I had worked for him for several years, he had no clue about my past. He never suspected that I was learning disabled or had been a behavior problem in both my schools and community. After I gave him the letter, he did not speak to me for almost a month. At first, I was concerned that my honesty had gotten me into trouble. Then he called me asking if he could share the letter with both of his daughters. What follows are some excerpts that I believe apply to those teachers who teach in the inner cities of America. They are especially relevant to teachers whose students appear to be in outer space rather than in a classroom.

I told her that as a consultant to her father he sometimes shared with me the frustration she experienced teaching. I explained that I understood her situation because I had been a student with characteristics similar to her students. I gave her a brief history of the problems I created both in the class and in my neighborhood. Then I said that there was good news:

"There comes a time when many 'bad' students wake up. At that time, they will not only remember the good teachers who tried to help them, but they will also remember many of the lessons they were taught. I speak from personal experience. I was considered dumb at best or a nuisance at worst and written off by most of those teachers. What none of my teachers knew in the late 1940's was that I was learning disabled. I wasn't dumb; I just could not read words or numbers that my mind tended to reverse. That's why I could not read out loud in class then—or even today."

The major point I made was that *"even so-called 'bad' kids appreciate sincere teachers."* Moreover, I said that she would be amazed if she knew how much her students will actually retain from her lessons even though they don't appear to be mentally present, let alone listening.

"I still remember poems read aloud in the 5th grade. Most of these kids will one day wake up, but that will be long after your years with them. So you are having an impact. When you are not dealing with 'good' students, it is easy to doubt the impact you are having on the so-called 'bad' students. Again, my point is that good teachers WILL have an impact well beyond their classroom years."

PARENTS WITH ADOLESCENT CHILDREN

The second category of parents who approach me are those with adolescent children who are not doing well in middle or high school and who appear to be without focus and in danger of not receiving a high school diploma.

Here my history is appropriate. Starting out as a high school dropout, I learned some valuable lessons that enabled me to succeed in a variety of settings. My original purpose for writing this book was to share the lessons learned with potential high school dropouts or those who have already dropped out of high school. Realizing that potential dropouts are not likely to read this book, my hope is that parents with children who fall into this category may find my experience useful in advising their children on some of the options that are available to them to help put their lives back together. The options I offer young people who have not performed well in school may not be what parents have in mind for their child, but they are still excellent options for young people to pursue because they speak to independence, financial security, and personal success for those who have not experienced any of these. Moreover, I offer them because they can provide a pathway for potential career objectives that parents want for their children.

Once I dropped out of high school, I soon discovered that I was not qualified to hold any job that paid more than minimum wage. I remember when the U.S. minimum wage was forty-five cents an hour. I saw it rise, over decades, to seventy-five cents, a dollar twenty-five, and to its current seven dollars and twenty-five cents. I learned that in the working world, the price of your wage is determined by the skills you bring to the job.

In my case, I possessed no marketable skills. I could barely read, write, or solve simple arithmetic problems. The only jobs I qualified for were those that required physical strength: loading and unloading trucks, delivering furniture, and driving small trucks. Some of my high school classmates went on to work in stores and businesses, went through management training programs, and found interesting work above minimum wage. Even those who started at minimum wage soon moved up the ladder in their companies, increasing their responsibilities and their pay. At the same time, most of my friends who quit school, like me, found themselves on a treadmill to nowhere. Some in my neighborhood stayed together after they left school, doing low-wage, boring work for which they qualified. The downside of that was that we reinforced each other's weaknesses by not meeting people in the mainstream who held good jobs and could have been our role models. Instead, we hung out on street corners and got into all sorts of trouble. Some engaged in crime, were caught and sent to prison. Others languished for decades standing on street corners watching people and automobiles pass by. We stood there for years, in winter or summer, rain or shine, just standing there.

Potential dropouts do not understand that once they are out of school, they will enter the real world, one in which everyone works in some form of a job. They may still be living at home, but once their middle school and high school years are behind them, they will have needs: clothes, automobiles, and spending money. Somehow, they must pay for these necessities of life.

When they are actively looking for a job, they will discover that their wages are determined by them. Employers hire people to perform services for which they pay a wage in accordance with the complexity of the tasks their employees are required to perform. But make no mistake, they will always be in the labor market; at the top, the middle, or the bottom—the choice is theirs. They can take any of the opportunities offered to them; the key is to examine their options.

CAREER OPTIONS FOR YOUNG ADULTS

In today's society, parents have been convinced that every child must go to college. Especially in middle class and upper middle communities, most parents want their children to go college and obtain a degree. But that may not be the road that their children initially select. If your child is not motivated to obtain a college degree, there are other very viable options they can pursue. If they have already dropped out of school and have no high school diploma, they should be encouraged to remedy that as soon as possible. The easiest option for a high-school dropout is receiving a GED certificate. With a GED in hand, they can enter a training program that can lead to meaningful employment. Such training programs may also lead to the possibility of attending community college, that will make them more valuable to their employer, increase their responsibility, and ultimately their pay. Many people begin working in a management training program and decide to move into a junior college or university because they see the advantage for even greater opportunity by obtaining a higher level of education and knowledge. But the first step with this option is obtaining a GED. To many employers, a GED demonstrates that such individuals are taking steps to become responsible.

Still another benefit is that many employers will pay employees to attend community college to learn skills that benefit their company. Work-related college courses will increase an employee's value to their employer and also make them more attractive in the labor market. Employer-sponsored college courses avoid the risk of accumulating debt while seeking a college degree that may not be focused on a market-based objective.

Over the last thirty years we have witnessed an enormous increase in students attending colleges and universities seeking the promised opportunity of upward economic and social mobility. But many of these college graduates have not found the meaningful careers or incomes they expected because they hold degrees in the liberal arts and humanities. In their twenties, many of these young adults are still living with their parents, which is not in keeping with their expectation for independence.

At the same time, many who have not gone to college but have entered apprenticeship programs have earning capacities well above the current crop of college degree holders. They are enjoying all the benefits college graduates expected, and they have incomes and company benefits that place them in the middle class. They own their own homes, automobiles, boats, campers, and their homes are filled with all the electronic wherewithal associated with the good life. I personally chose this option when I entered an apprenticeship to obtain an optical license. There are dozens of other industries that offer a career path to anyone seeking to learn a trade or craft, whether it be as a carpenter, electrician, auto mechanic, cosmetologist, brick and stone mason, or welder. All of these crafts require becoming an apprentice under the guidance of a master craftsman. In today's marketplace, there are also a wide range of opportunities in the technology field.

OPPORTUNITIES IN THE MILITARY

Still other opportunities exist in programs offered by the military. In my dealings with the Pentagon and in private industry, I encounter many officials who developed marketable skills they learned while in the service. Since the nation moved to a volunteer service, the military has offered both men and women enlistees opportunities to attend college as a benefit for the time they serve in the military. Job requirements in the military offer personnel the chance to master computer skills and technical knowledge that are found in the private sector. In my business, I often work with former military personnel in private corporations who transferred the training and experience they gained in the military into high paying civilian jobs.

Given my horrible track record in the National Guard, you might ask why I would recommend the military to someone else since it was the apprenticeship that gave me the discipline to move up the ladder into other areas. The answer is because the military offers the element of discipline which many high school students lack. The military makes adults out of children. It also offers career opportunities and promotions to higher rank not found in the private sector. It should not be overlooked that the military offers young people leadership positions generally not available in the private sector. I was too immature at the time to appreciate these opportunities, but that, by no means, is a reason for others to disregard military service.

The essential element for success in all of the opportunities available for older children is their commitment to apply themselves to mastering those essentials required of the job or the profession. There are options for youngsters who lack motivation in school, but they must be willing to take the opportunity offered to them. Parents can help them make these career choices.

Chapter 5

The Role of the School Counselor

During elementary and middle school, parents usually monitor the relationship between their children and their teachers very closely. In high school, students are often treated as young adults. Many have their own automobiles and are given much more freedom than they had in earlier school years. However, this is the period of time when students are expected to choose what career paths they will take after graduation. It is at this point that the role of school counselor becomes critical.

In my grammar school years during the 1940s and 50s, some teachers were also guidance counselors who tried to advise students on career paths. But many were primarily disciplinarians whose job it was to monitor troublemakers like me until we were old enough to leave school. In my day, high school courses divided students into those who were expected to go on to college or business school and those who would pass on into the non-college workforce. The non-college track students received little counseling; they simply entered the local economy and found employment.

Today the preface "guidance" has been removed from the word counselor. No longer are the counselors drawn from classroom teachers; instead, they have undergraduate degrees in counseling as well as master's degrees. Their role has been transformed from disciplinarian to career counselors who recommend that students take courses that will prepare them for college after graduation or for entrance into the job market.

Over the last four decades, I have counseled students on career goals and objectives. I have also lectured undergraduate and graduate students in several universities and an eight-week private seminar that I held in my corporation focusing on economics and political theory. Attendees were excellent students from private schools. They were identified early in life as the students who would attend college and postgraduate institutions. In their young lives they had the good fortune of being raised by parents who supported them emotionally, intellectually, and financially. Most were from suburban communities where parents and professionals paved the way for their children to follow in their footsteps. Most of these students were not a problem to their parents, their teachers, or their communities. They were in advanced programs and took prep courses to enable them to make the highest scores on the pre-college entrance exams that would help them be accepted into the college of their choice.

These, of course, are the best students. But what about students like me whose parents were not able to provide them with the resources that students from middle class families transfer to their children? Schools across America are filled with these children. It is sufficient to say that in many inner-city schools there is a large portion of the student body who will not be taking the prep courses for college entrance requirements. In fact, many of these students will probably not complete high school. Moreover, in inner-city schools like those I attended, counselors are not focusing on college entrance exams; they are dealing with discipline problems with students who are most likely not going to graduate.

Thankfully, today we have a new generation of young teachers filled with idealism and eager to teach in inner-city schools. Yet many are frustrated because their teaching credentials are not geared to dealing with the non-performers in their classes.

Getting inner-city students to graduate from high school is an important objective. Still, many of these graduates will have a diploma but will not have mastered the skills necessary to improve their social and economic status in the working world. For what kind of jobs will these young people qualify? Hopefully, they will be able to read and write, solve basic math problems, and have some knowledge of world history. But our economy is now a global one that is focused on computer skills, marketing, sales, finance, and public employment jobs that are increasingly filled with college graduates. Where will our non-college, high school graduates work?

There is one sector of the economy that is wide open and begging for young people to enter. What is more, it is open to high school graduates and even high school dropouts who want to become financially independent and part of America's middle class. I refer to the sector of the economy that is found in the crafts and trades in the vocational arts.

In the 1940s and 1950s, the public schools offered vocational training. In addition to the academic subjects, there were courses in woodworking, printing, plastic, metal, electrical and auto repair shops. They were not full apprenticeships that led to a journeyman status, but they did provide an introduction to the numerous trades that one might pursue after high school. In addition, there were trade schools that offered both high school diplomas as well as certificates that enabled trade school graduates to move into any of the trades or crafts.

For whatever reason, the public schools have for the most part stopped offering these programs. Instead, the emphasis has been placed on acquiring a college degree. The focus of public education has shifted to getting all students into college. It has become socially desirable, and therefore competitive, to possess a college degree. Hence, it is not surprising that over time a college education compared more favorably to the less attractive picture of grease and grime under the fingernails of the working class. There seemed to be a belief that the American workforce of tomorrow would be comprised of degree-holding college graduates who would dominate the nation's workforce. During this same period, there was a de-escalation of efforts in our middle and high schools to introduce students to the opportunities in the vocational arts. Furthermore, over the last 40 years, no one seemed to notice that the manufacturing sector of our economy—that always provided Americans with a path to the middle class—was collapsing. American educators seemed unaware of the disappearance of trade schools, apprenticeship programs, and vocational education programs that provided a sizable majority of the jobs of the working class. Few educators—as well as the general public—would admit there was and still is a prejudice in favor of the college educated as opposed to those engaged in manual labor.

During this time the role of guidance and school counselors changed from my day when guidance counselors came from the ranks of teachers who dealt with problem students like me. Today they are credentialed professionals who help students choose high school courses, study for the college entrance exams, select appropriate colleges and decide on career choices.

Then came the development of an entire cottage industry of counselors in the private sector to aid students in their college choices as well as preparing them for the exams. High school students were prepared for college entrance exams along with evidence that they were engaged in all of those volunteer activities that presented a socially, as well as academically, desirable candidate. And so, it went through the decades with the cost of college education going through the roof. These costs were ignored because high paying, meaningful careers were almost guaranteed if one possessed a college degree. Everyone now sees how far off the mark that strategy was. Today we have the largest number of unemployed, degree-holding generalists in our history. We have seen them on TV and in demonstrations everywhere from Wall Street to Seattle complaining that the system let them down. No one has fully analyzed the problem, but it is clear the majority of these unemployed graduates hold degrees for which there are no jobs. On one weekend talk show, a group of students were interviewed about their inability to find a job. One young woman admitted that she created her own major.[8] The problem was that there is no employment opportunity that coincided with her major. We now have some 40 million degree-holders with a collective debt of $1.5 trillion, many of whom live at home and cannot find a job.[9]

Through the 1980s and 1990s, it became clear that education was falling short of the promise that there was a place for everyone in the American workforce. At this same time the public began to notice the disappearance of manufacturing jobs. Missing were those jobs normally associated with apprenticeship programs that produced craftsmen with skills associated with vocational education. These apprenticeships were proven pathways to middle class. Today public policy makers are recognizing the need to offer grade school and middle school students the opportunity to explore the skills training found in vocational education. In our modern economy these careers are not given the same high regard as white collar jobs sought after by college graduates.

One cannot discuss the difference between a career that requires a college degree and the skills required in the crafts or vocational arts without a frank discussion about the stereotypes people have of employees in either profession. From the earliest days in the republic, the workforce could be divided into white-collar and blue-collar employees. White-collar employees—doctors, engineers, scientists, lawyers, business executives, accountants—do not engage in physical labor or get their hands dirty. Over time there developed an unconscious bias about the fact that industrial workers were characterized by greasy hands ("Joe Greasy Paw"). Further, there developed the view that the white-collar class—especially those with a college degree—were somehow superior to the factory worker class because they had a college degree.

When talking about doctors, lawyers, engineers, and scientists, one can argue that mastering any of these disciplines requires years of study and a fair degree of intelligence. But that is not true of all those who hold a college degree. In fact, the requirement for a college degree has now become somewhat commonplace. Still there is a "greasy paw" view of industrial workers that persists today.

Mike Rowe, an actor and producer of television documentaries on working-class occupations, has testified before numerous congressional committees on the need to appreciate the dignity of those who work the "Dirty Jobs." Rowe's focus is on the skills gap: the shortage of people willing to work in manual labor jobs. Following his testimony before a House Congressional Committee on March 1, 2017, Rowe pointed to an attitude prevalent among educators that negatively compared vocational education careers with the prestige associated with possessing a college degree.

Rowe argued that US schools have taken vocational education and skill crafts out of high school at the same time that we have told an entire generation their best hope for success is a four-year degree. Rowe then pointed out that there is a massive lobby of front-line guidance counselors who incentivized higher education as opposed to careers associated with the skills and crafts requiring vocational education. Vocational education is neither being incentivized nor celebrated. We have pushed an entire generation into holding college degrees for which there are fewer high paying and satisfying careers.

Rowe noted that students are encouraged to take the "most expensive" path as a career option where the cost of a college education has increased more than inflation, healthcare, real estate, or any other commodity in our economy. Additionally, of the 5.6 million jobs open in our economy, 75 percent do not require a college education. The skills gap has been compounded by the reduction of manufacturing jobs because of US trade and tax policies that incentivize manufacturers to move their facilities to foreign countries, reducing employment throughout that sector of our economy. This has resulted in a re-examination of how Americans for most of the 20th century climbed the economic ladder and made it into the middle class. They did so not by relying only on college degrees but by working in the trades and crafts learned through quality vocational programs and apprenticeship programs. These were the conveyor belt to the middle class.[10]

Throughout the country there appears to be an awakening of the need to recreate that work environment where skills are honored. There are a few that are worth noting. The small town of Steubenville, Ohio, was once considered an industrial center. The output of its steel mills ranked alongside those in Youngstown, Pittsburg and Gary, Indiana. Mills in the Tri-City area of Steubenville, Wheeling, West Virginia, and Western Pennsylvania that once employed tens of thousands of steelworkers now employ a few hundred steel workers. The community searches for a future for its young people.

In 1975 the community established the Jefferson County Joint Vocational School. The school provides training that enables students to receive certification in electrical work, auto repair, welding, nursing, and healthcare services. Students are enrolled in the vocational school through local high schools. Upon completion of their coursework, students are awarded a high school diploma. Only juniors and seniors are enrolled in this program. School counselors and teachers reach out to local businesses to help place students in jobs. The interaction between local businesses and industrial companies in the area helps to assess the skilled personnel needed in the area and the courses taught in the school. This is an excellent model for both rural and inner-city schools to emulate, as it provides jobs along with a high school diploma.

In Wisconsin, Sheboygan South High School created a co-op program with local manufacturers to identify the skills needed by companies in the area. Company officials saw the school's outdated equipment and donated $5.2 million to provide modern equipment and updated curriculum, thereby making it relevant to modern manufacturing. In 2016, the school and local manufacturers launched a paid 90-hour career exploration opportunity in their facility. The students are exposed to all aspects of company skill needs, including accounting, engineering, research, and design. Students see the opportunity for a meaningful career with a paying job right after high school, rather than paying tens of thousands of dollars for a college degree without a job prospect.[11]

Still another approach to offering students career opportunities in manufacturing was initiated by Huntington Ingalls Industries. This company is the nation's premier shipbuilder of nuclear aircraft carriers and submarines as well as conventional ships for the Coast Guard. The company has built Navy ships for almost a hundred years. Its Newport News facility in Virginia established an apprentice school the day the yard was opened. It has built warships that defended America throughout all the wars of the 20th century, as it does today. Throughout the decades, generations of workers seeking high-paying jobs were attracted to its shipyards because of its wages and benefits. During World War I and the Great Depression, the yard provided a decent living for skilled and unskilled workers eager to begin a career in manufacturing.

In the early days, the yard had to compete for workers who had opportunities in other manufacturing facilities in our industrial economy. But, in more recent times, the manufacturing sector appeared in decline. The reduction in opportunities in the manufacturing sector coincided with the attraction of middle and high school students to obtaining a career that required a college degree. Again, it seemed more attractive to avoid the jobs that appeared to be associated with manual labor. The trend toward promoting a college career rather than an apprenticeship for employment in the manufacturing sector is widely recognized today. The usual reference made by teachers and counselors was to tell their students they had "better get their grades up or else." "Or else" generally referred to a manual labor job in the industrial sector of our economy.

In a 2016 keynote address at the Washington Press Club on the Future of Manufacturing, Mike Petters, President and CEO of Huntington Ingalls Industries, said that the company would be investing $1.5 billion over the next five years to improve performance.[12] He noted that the title of Master Shipbuilder is reserved for those who have had unbroken service in a yard for 40 years, Petters added that there are 1,000 Master Shipbuilders at Huntington Ingalls where shipbuilders from three generations have found steady, meaningful work and are part of the middle class.

Petters said that the biggest selling point for entrance into the apprenticeship program is the ability to earn while you learn. "At our two apprentice schools, we offer tuition-free training in a wide variety of shipbuilding disciplines, from welding and pipefitting to dimensional control and nuclear testing." First-year apprentices at both schools earn close to $35,000 with automatic raises that are built in over the life of the apprenticeship. Petters told the audience, "Of the 4,000 applicants, only 220 are admitted each year, a rate that rivals Harvard and Yale."

Mindful of the stereotype of dirty hands, Petters challenged the description usually applied to manufacturing workers as "metal benders" saying that, over five generations, the intellectual requirements for shipyard workers have increased and now require more brains than brawn. He then cited the requirements for a job in the yard: "Must be proficient in math, algebra, physics. Candidate must understand summation of moments. This is a four-step process to determine center of gravity." He then asked his learned audience, "Can you do that?" and went on to say, "Candidate should also be able to use trigonometry . . . and use geometry to calculate load weight." He added, "You might think these are the requirements for a designer, planner or even an engineer, but they are actually for a rigger." Riggers are skilled trades workers who hook up loads and signal cranes to pick up and move components to locations aboard ship. "So, the stakes in shipbuilding are high, and the requirements to land even an entry-level job are pretty steep."[13]

A TEACHER INTERN PROGRAM

Realizing that teachers and school counselors might view employment in a shipyard as less attractive than recommending to students that they go to college, Petters chose an innovative approach to educating local science, technology, engineering and math (STEM) teachers. He created a paid sabbatical in the yard during the summer recess in which teachers and counselors are exposed to the preparation given to apprentices in math, physics, and engineering. The program, called The Teacher Internship Program, gives school personnel an opportunity to witness firsthand modern manufacturing techniques that shatter the myth of "greasy paw metal benders."

The management at Huntington Ingalls Industries believes that jobs in their shipyard offer ambitious students careers that pay salaries equal to or better than jobs requiring a college degree. The Teacher Internship Program is designed to educate teachers and school counselors about opportunities available in the shipyard, opportunities perfectly acceptable both to students who are qualified for college and students who are not expected to go on to college.

During each session, teacher interns are exposed to all facets of shipbuilding including engineering, modeling, simulation and hands-on experience with trades. Participants have the opportunity to experience engineering programs, real and virtual reality modeling, and simulation. They observe workers building aircraft carriers and submarines. They also examine the courses that are offered in the apprentice school. The teacher participants are immersed in different job functions across the shipyard to experience the competency required by the workforce and how these competencies relate directly to the courses taught in the high schools. They examine all of the crafts and trades taught in the shipyards: piping, welding, electronics, mechanics, and radiological controls—all skills taught in the apprenticeship school.

Bringing the teachers and counselors into an actual work setting during ship construction enables them to recognize how math and science concepts used in the yard relate to what they are teaching in the classroom. They are exposed to the vast career opportunities available in the shipyard through the apprenticeship school. The goal is to have program participants return to their schools to:

- Share their story/experiences with peers, students, and parents.
- Emphasize the degreed and non-degreed opportunities available to their students.
- Steer talent in the right direction based on where they show aptitude.
- Develop the relationship between the higher sciences and math to all aspects of shipbuilding (from craftsman to engineer).

At the conclusion of the internship, each teacher is required to present a marketing skit for their students, parents, and fellow teachers. So far, 120 teachers and counselors have completed the internship program since it began in 2012.

Through the Career Pathways Teacher Intern program, Huntington Ingalls partners with public school systems to mentor both students and teachers to enrich school curricula. Specifically designed for teachers and counselors, this fulltime internship allows selected middle and high school educators to gain insights throughout the different programs and trades by experiencing what craftsmen—such as welders, pipe fitters, and electricians—actually do in building and maintaining Navy ships. The educators will be able to incorporate their new knowledge in future lesson plans to help students prepare for careers in shipbuilding, manufacturing, and other STEM-related fields.

To assess the impact of the program, I interviewed some of the recent graduates. One was a counselor at a middle school and two others were high school math teachers. The middle school counselor noted that her group was actually moved to tears when they experienced the pride displayed by craftsmen throughout the yard. A male high school math teacher was able to find clear messages to share with his students. "It gave many of us a stronger case to make to our students about the need to master basic math concepts that are applied by workers in the shipyard on a daily basis."

Another former math teacher was most enthusiastic about her experience. Ms. Kari Egnot is the Division Director of Testing in the Newport Public School System, where she oversees 42 schools that include elementary, middle, and high schools for national state and local test administrations. Her observations are insightful. She noted that the internship helped her answer student questions concerning the relevance of formulas and equations used in solving problems in the classroom. "The question we always, always get when we introduce a math concept is 'How will we ever use any of these math formulas?' Because of my experience in the shipyard, I was able to respond with confidence that 'this information I am presenting today will help to build your career. Don't focus on the mathematical formula we are presenting to you; focus on the rules behind the math.'" She noted that the riggers were her favorite because they were using the trigonometry to move objects. They understood that if they moved the object in this direction, all the other angles changed accordingly. "So, to answer your question as to how the internship affected me," she said, "when I came back to the classroom, I was able to tell my students that they will be able to use this information that I give them to solve problems. I tell them that math doesn't teach you to solve formulas; it teaches you how to think, how to respond to problem solving."

She added, "We put up bulletin boards showing how each of the crafts practiced in the yard had a corresponding math skill that accompanied it. As a math teacher, I was able to demonstrate the relevance of math to real life situations."

This effort has now changed the advice teachers offer their students. From "If you don't get your grades up, you will wind up in the shipyard," to, "If you don't get your grades up, you will NOT get into that shipyard." Throughout life in general, it is important for people to understand at least basic math. As a teen, I once worked for a company that advertised on billboards throughout the state. I started out by changing burned-out light bulbs, but the company wanted me to learn how to wire the billboards. That required me to attend a local trade school at night to learn basic wiring. I survived two classes in elementary electronics, but I could not do the basic math that would have helped me keep the job, so I left the sign company.

Finally, on the stereotype of dirty jobs generally associated with industrial careers, David Goodreau of the Small Manufacturers Association of California argues that modern manufacturing is no longer dirty. Goodreau argues manufacturing has been evolving toward clean, organized, and automated environments over the last thirty years. In his experience, he claims that when he has the opportunity to showcase today's reality with a shop floor tour to academic or political representatives, they are speechless to describe the disconnect between the clean, modern facility they see with the historical storyline of old, dirty, dead-end manufacturing jobs. He believes that the media has aided this perception by not keeping up with current realities on the shop floor that is quite opposite of what has been portrayed. In a recent interview, Goodreau said, "You should see the light bulbs go on when students tour today's manufacturing plant. It is amazing how this career sector has changed students' lives when they witness alternatives to 'book learning' through the application of knowledge within a manufacturing career."

This is a far cry from my brief period at Barnum Machine Company where I shoveled oil-soaked steel chips from beneath a machine and the days when my father made us laugh by talking about wallowing in oil.

Goodreau is convinced that the strongest way to alter this anti-manufacturing perception is through apprenticeship programs. This time-tested model is adaptable to the times and is simply a commitment between two parties to share in the benefit from their growth. Apprenticeships enable small companies to reach out in their communities and empower students and young adults to embrace their innate "hands-on" characteristics that can link them to satisfying career choices in manufacturing.

However, it is important to understand that all of the crafts in manufacturing require a basic understanding of the skills supposedly learned in high school. Yet, many of those who have completed high school lack the basic English and math skills required for the entry level into apprentice programs.

This local problem is validated in the recent 2018 report, "Too Big to Fail: Millennials on the Margins," that describes the problem as follows: "Out of a cohort of 77 million millennials, 36 million have low skills in literacy and 46 million in numeracy."[14] These statistics point to strategic weaknesses within and outside the existing workforce from academic weaknesses that create stealth-like barriers to corporate, personal and career growth.

THE CHANGING FOCUS OF EDUCATION

Today we are witnessing a shift in the selection of college courses away from math, science, and engineering programs to the humanities. When John Kennedy set a goal of landing on the moon, an entire generation of students was motivated to study math, science and engineering. By the late 1960s, the number of engineers and scientists graduating with advanced degrees surpassed all other periods in our history.

Then came the cuts in space exploration and the expectation of job opportunities that warranted the enormous effort required to obtain engineering degrees. This was accompanied by the expansion of college courses in the humanities. These subjects include sociology, psychology, political science, elementary and secondary education, and subjects such as women's studies, ethnic studies and gender studies.

Norman Augustine, former Chairman of Lockheed Martin who wrote the foreword to this book, is regarded as a giant in engineering. He has headed presidential commissions on a variety of scientific problems and has devoted his life to promoting engineering programs both at the undergraduate and postgraduate levels. Augustine has been quite vocal concerning the reduction of graduates in engineering, science, and math programs. In a 2009 editorial titled "Race to the Bottom" published in the prestigious aerospace magazine, *Aviation Week and Space Technology*, he wrote of his concern about the relevance of engineering programs to the health of our economy. He noted that engineers account for only 4% of the nation's workforce but create the jobs for the other 96% of the population. He pointed to the shift of students from more difficult course curricula in engineering to the humanities—courses that do not require the intellectual effort to obtain a degree.[15] He quoted an article in the *Washington Post* that asked the question, "How do you get good grades in college?" The Post suggested, "Don't study engineering."

Augustine concluded that courses are now being taught by teachers who have teaching degrees but lack the comprehensive knowledge in the subjects they teach. "Students in grades 5-8 have a 69% chance of having a math teacher who does not have a degree in math, and 93% chance of a having a science teacher not having a degree in science."

In his editorial, Augustine noted, "We seem unwilling to embrace revolutionary notions that physics teachers should perhaps be paid more than physical education teachers; that good teachers might be paid more than mediocre ones; and that physics teachers might be paid as much as football coaches."

Being a true steward of society, Augustine decided he would leave his position as CEO of one of the nation's major aerospace companies to teach in a local high school. He immediately ran into an invisible wall that prevents outsiders from teaching in a public school if they do not have a college degree in teaching. An incredibly gifted mathematician was deemed unqualified to teach math in any public school in his state. This would be like preventing Plato or Aristotle from teaching a course in government or civics because they did not have a teaching degree.

Fortunately, Princeton University had a greater appreciation of his talents and offered him a position on the faculty. Students ranked his course as one of ten that every student at Princeton should take before graduating.

Augustine advocates that there is a national need for encouraging graduates in math and engineering. You can see why there is a movement to private schools. Whether teaching a class about skilled trades, or teaching engineering and math, the average public school teacher may be ill-prepared to advise students about the labor market or the competitive world of engineering. Engineering scholars like Norm Augustine can enhance classroom instruction but are not welcome to do so in the public high schools.

Let me clarify that I am not opposed to students pursuing degrees in the liberal arts or humanities. I have an undergraduate degree in history and a PhD in classical political theory. At the same time, as a nation, we are falling behind in engineering, math and science, and could use the help of industrialists who would take a leave of absence to allow them to teach in our schools where need is clearly apparent.

Augustine and others lobbied for the Congress to provide $100 million to subsidize the salary of engineers willing to teach in public schools, with the subsidy tied to performance. He laments that the nation's largest teachers union strongly opposed this proposal, which resulted in its being defeated.

In the 2009 editorial Augustine concluded that, since students cannot speak for themselves, their eventual employers need to do so as a social obligation and out of corporate self-interest. "Every CEO in America should be writing op-eds, and attending school board meetings, hopefully in the company of union leaders who represent the employees." It is all about jobs.

Those who are in charge of educational policy in this country should seek the appropriate help where needed. It is likely that the industrial community will eventually make the case, but a solution must be found. What is needed is a creative partnership between industry and public education. Surely something can be structured to reduce the gap and to help our students and satisfy our educators.

Having said what we have about past and current school counselors who favor helping high school students to continue on to college, one must be sympathetic to the pressure that parents put upon them. Parents do not want to hear that their children are not college material. If college is seen as the only path to wealth and status in America, how do school counselors tell parents that college is not for their child? To those teachers and counselors not wanting to offend parents, I would urge them to offer the temporary alternative of an apprenticeship in a craft as an interim step to help the student use that time to develop the discipline and insights needed for success. I say this because a student may need that time to obtain a better assessment of themselves, to succeed in one area before attempting another. In my case, no one, myself included, would have believed that when I left high school I would one day earn an undergraduate degree, let alone a PhD. The optical apprenticeship allowed me an intellectual moratorium where I developed the discipline and self-respect I needed. Success as an apprentice showed me that I could pursue other careers. In this regard it is important to recognize that counselors play a critical role in the process. They are the last stop. Whatever teachers have been able to accomplish with students in terms of identifying their skills and their dreams, counselors will ultimately have the greatest impact on their lives. They direct students to what they believe is the most appropriate career path.

Chapter 6

The Apprenticeship Revolution

Whether the result of trade policies, outsourcing, or globalism, for the past 50 years our industrial base has been eroding. The industrial base that allowed America to fight all the wars of the 20th century, including World War II that was fought in two hemispheres, has now been seriously undermined. Adjusting our corporate tax policy to equal that of our competitors has now created a level global playing field. Consequently, today there is a renewed interest in restoring America's manufacturing industrial base. Corporations large and small are looking for people interested in working in industries that build everything from giant ships to titanium dental implants. These jobs require multi-year apprenticeships and years of on-the-job training.

Apprenticeships can be found in a wide variety of fields that range from the basic skilled trades that include carpenters, electricians, plumbers and masons. Apprenticeships are also available in the rapidly growing industrial sector in the machine tool industry and manufacturing where modern machines are operated by workers with computer skills.

In short, the market is wide open to people who are willing to enter an apprenticeship program of some kind in a variety of industries. Most of these apprenticeships offer good starting salaries as well as benefits such as healthcare and paid vacation, so one can earn while they learn. But there are many other benefits that come with an apprenticeship program.

Apprenticeships build character

Learning a trade requires the apprentice to tolerate being at the entry level. An apprenticeship will require one to carry boards and fetch tools, carry pipe, and be responsible for cleaning up after the job. Like all other endeavors, success means taking orders and learning from the master craftsman. Learning a trade was the path I took. I progressed through my optical apprenticeship from one degree of complexity to another. I devoted the time needed to study, not only on the job but on nights and weekends. My goal was to master every part of my job. Becoming an optician meant understanding the anatomy and physiology of the eye as well as the physics of how light and images pass through a lens, striking the retina, and enabling a person to see. Sounds complicated? It is. But your child can understand it by breaking the theory down into smaller components that make the theory understandable.

Apprenticeships teach structure

To learn anything, one must start at the beginning. Apprenticeships offer a beginner the opportunity to learn how to take orders. The master craftsman supervising and mentoring the apprentice had to learn exactly what the apprentice will learn. Master craftsmen give orders because they learned to take orders. Taking orders could be a major change in your child's life. Many high-school students never master the discipline of taking orders.

Apprenticeships instill self-discipline

For some, an apprenticeship is the first step in developing responsibility like getting up in the morning and showing up on time for work. I lost many jobs when I showed up late for work. Today I realize that my absence delayed the starting time for other workers as well.

Apprenticeships create confidence (self-respect)

Finally, an apprenticeship can change your child's life. In the different phases of work that they are required to master, they will develop a sense of pride in their accomplishments. They will earn the respect of their trainers and co-workers. Equally important, they will begin to respect themselves. That was my experience in the optical apprenticeship. The same will be true for any of the other crafts that require phases of learning. Whether it be welding a pipe for a nuclear submarine, or installing all of the plumbing for a hotel, not only will they be paid but they will be respected for what they build and how it is useful to other people.

Once they begin to climb the steps up the ladder in an apprenticeship, new opportunities will appear. In my case, I went from a lens grinder, to managing lens grinders, to department head, to obtaining an optical license, to becoming a branch manager of an optical company and eventually being offered a partnership in that company. I chose to attend a university, graduated from college, went on to graduate school and was awarded a PhD, worked at the White House, managed a federal agency and founded my own company. None of this would have happened had I not entered an optical apprenticeship on the lowest rung of the ladder, earning less than fifty cents an hour.

EXPANDING CAREER OPTIONS
FOR ALL STUDENTS

Looking at student populations in America's middle and high schools, most teachers know which students are likely not to go to college. These are students who may graduate but will most likely not have the skills for jobs that pay above the minimum wage. It was to address the needs of these students that the crafts or trades were taught in public schools for almost 50 years. Any educational system seeking to provide a full range of career options for all students must respond to the needs of a society, and must be able to provide a spectrum of teachers and instructors with appropriate knowledge and expertise.

Our public schools once exposed students to the crafts, trades, and vocational arts. Today, there are fewer and fewer teachers in public schools who offer education in the industrial arts. Given the expanding opportunities opening in our industrial economy, there is a need for teachers who can at least introduce students to the new opportunities now available. The crafts we have been considering are not likely to be taught in colleges offering a degree in education. They will have to come from the industrial disciplines where they now reside.

Where does one find a cadre of carpenters, welders, plumbers, etc., needed and willing to teach in public schools? They are likely to be engaged in the trades. It is also likely that most of these people will not have college credentials required by state governments today. Utilizing the skills of these craftsmen in a classroom may require relaxing current state and local requirements that one must have a college degree to teach in a public school.

I suspect that many of the teachers who taught "shop" in public schools actually received a degree in education. While they taught in the plastic or metal, or print shop, it is not likely that these shop teachers were craftsmen who could enter the trades professionally. Nonetheless, they were good teachers and did an excellent job of introducing students to the availability of opportunity in the industrial sector. Today our needs are more immediate. We need to restart the process now.

As noted in the previous chapter, the eminently qualified engineer and mathematician, Norm Augustine, was prevented from teaching math in a high school in his state because he did not have a teaching degree. Augustine sought to volunteer to teach fulltime in a high school to motivate students to go on to college to obtain a degree in math. Apparently, the current system of education is based on the notion that only those with a college degree in education are qualified to teach. If schools were more flexible, they would allow math/science experts to demonstrate not only that they are knowledgeable in a given subject area, but also that they can write a lesson plan as required by the state department of education.

As the director of a national association of industrial workers that includes unions from the crafts to engineers and scientists, I know there are people like Augustine, nearing retirement, who would jump at the chance to help the next generation. In the engineering community, the average worker has an advanced degree so that at least they would meet the threshold of being educated people who are familiar with college curriculums, taking and passing exams. Augustine's example notwithstanding, I am sure the public would support using skilled craftsmen and engineers who are motivated by their idealism to teach in the public schools.

Not every trade is the same in terms of the complexity of the skills that must be mastered. For example, when people think of welders, they usually conjure up visions of people wearing masks, using an acetylene torch and sparks flying as steel is welded. But there are many other metals that require additional expertise. In the space program, for example, different techniques are used to weld different grades of beryllium. In the shipbuilding program, yet other skills are required to weld pipes on nuclear aircraft carriers and submarines. These welders are trained for at least six years before they are qualified as experts. Many of these craftsmen can teach or motivate students even though they do not have a college degree.

In doing research for this book, I learned of a welding program taught at Red Mountain High School in Mesa, Arizona. Daniel Hurst has been in charge of that program for more than five years. As a child he grew up near a rural airstrip used by biplane crop dusters. He watched the local craftsmen servicing equipment and was attracted to a career in welding. Being a welder for most of his life, in 2013 he began teaching welding at a local community college, and then at Red Mountain High School.

Hurst believes that not all high school-age students will follow the current trend to obtain a college degree and that "our youth need other paths to follow. I look into the eyes of our youth and see the future. It is up to us to make it happen."

Hurst expresses pride in the impact he has had on students he has taught at the high school. One of his students, Chase Diersen, studied advanced welding at the Lincoln Electrical School of Welding in Cleveland, Ohio, where he obtained 15 American Welding School certifications. Following graduation, Diersen returned to Mesa where he started his own welding company. He has begun to make an impact on the local community by hiring a welder who graduated from another high school in the area. Recognizing the expanding market, Diersen has begun to expand his company to address the need.

Since there is a growing need for welders, Hurst states that craftsmen and women who would be willing to teach in our schools should be allowed to do so. He points out that the American Welders Society now predicts a shortage of 400,000 welders by 2024, thus resulting in the US falling behind in this crucial art.

There are many such careers in the industrial arts that could be opened to high school graduates if state departments of education had more flexible rules with respect to requiring academic credentials. We have to find a way to accelerate allowing non-college instructors like Daniel Hurst to get into the high schools and provide alternative career opportunities for students who will not be going to college.

Looking at craftsmen and women in the basic trades, it is also likely that many people will not have college credentials acceptable to educators in some states. Here, too, there are crafts in the basic trades whose complexities are not fully appreciated by the general public. For example, most people think about plumbers as people who service broken pipes in their house. True. But plumbers also construct plumbing in multistory high-rise office buildings requiring thousands of connections in sinks, bathrooms and air-conditioning systems. The same is true for electricians who are viewed as wiring electrical outlets in domestic housing. Yet, electrical work involves a great deal more complexity, such as the wiring in major hotels, office buildings, and industrial facilities. Such activity goes far beyond the wiring we did for advertising billboards for the Art Sign Company.

As indicated in earlier chapters, both the teachers and those who work in the most skilled areas in the basic trades are union members. So, it is likely that both the state laws and union rules may become a considerable obstacle for allowing non-college personnel to teach in the public schools. At the same time, we have a need and no short-term solution to meeting that need. From my dealing with unions in the basic trades I know the unions in the crafts along with unions who represent engineers and scientists want to help educate the next generation.

When I became Director of the Peace Corps, a majority of our volunteers deployed in host countries were BA generalists. They taught English as a foreign language and provided basic health services in village communities. Because of my relationship with craft unions, I introduced the placement of retired union craftsmen into our volunteer profile to establish training in the basic trades. These included carpentry, plumbing, masonry and other crafts. While all of these craftsmen were experts in their chosen fields, none had teaching credentials. They were all products of apprenticeship programs. The host government never questioned their ability to teach their crafts. Moreover, they were not prevented from teaching because they did not have college degrees. Host governments were more than happy to provide their populations with the skills needed to advance the economic viability of their citizens.

There will be those who will argue that academic credentials are a basic requirement for teaching. When I have raised the subject of non-credentialed craftsmen and women, I have been told that the state requires a lesson plan to evaluate teaching materials. But from my experience as an apprentice myself and all of those apprentices I know, our belief is that an apprenticeship is itself a lesson plan, with each new component building on the previous.

Other obstacles could include the absence of machinery needed for training students. When I attended shop class in the 1940s there were very few machines in the labs. These were basic tools used in production. In the woodworking shop, for example, there was a band saw, a jig saw, a drill press, and a lathe. Operating any of these machines was under the direct supervision of the instructor. This was also true in the metal, plastic and electric shops. All of those machines were inexpensive and were basic in any woodworking or metal shop.

The machinery used in modern manufacturing is clean, safe and very expensive. The argument will be, "Where will school systems get the money to buy these machines?" Here a creative partnership with local businesses could provide the initial funds for the school to obtain that machinery. Local industries could receive a tax credit to provide the essential machinery necessary for teaching in public schools. Earlier in this book we cited an example of a high school in Sheboygan, Wisconsin. A creative partnership between local businesses, local industries, and local schools provided the machinery needed in the classroom. A similar program exists in a marine repair facility located in Beaufort, South Carolina. In this case students leave high school and attend classes in the industrial facility. It is also possible for students to receive training by companies offering students to come to their facilities during fixed time periods and receive high school credit toward their diploma. Not all students will apply for such programs. But those who would, should have that opportunity.

There is also a need to recreate or expand institutions once called trade schools. In New Haven, Connecticut, there was one called Boardman Trade School. It was located between two existing high schools a block apart. My guitar teacher, Frank D'Amato, graduated from Boardman with a certificate in mechanical drawing. He could have gone on to be draftsman, but instead chose a career in music. One of my grammar school classmates, Alex DePino, who attended a woodworking class with me, attended Boardman Trade School to study carpentry. When he graduated, he started his own construction company.

In both the shop classes in middle school and at Boardman Trade, the attendees did not receive journeyman's status. They received a basic education in theory and limited practice. When they left Boardman, they worked at jobs which required them to maintain the status of apprentice. This is important in all trades and crafts. Remember, when a doctor graduates from medical school, he or she begins training in a hospital for two or more years to get the experience needed to continue a career in medicine. All professions have a learning curve in order to achieve mastery.

Yes, there will be obstacles, but the opportunities will be worth the struggle to overcome them. What is needed is a creative partnership between industry and public education. Surely something can be structured to allow skilled craftsmen to satisfy a basic need in our high schools to provide all of our young people with a wider range of career options.

Apprenticeship programs offer a wide range of career options for all students. In my case, despite my dyslexia and other learning disabilities, the optical apprenticeship enabled a high school dropout to begin a journey that led to my earning a good living and later attending college and graduate school. Apprenticeships in any of the crafts are open to dyslexics or learning disabled students. They are also open to students who will graduate from high school without specific career goals. Apprenticeships offer more opportunities than the minimum wage jobs one finds in the general economy. Finally, apprenticeships are open to high school graduates who possess all the requirements needed to enter college but have not settled on career objectives they would pursue after college. An apprenticeship allows for growth and maturing while earning a living and using the time to determine whether college is the right path to follow.

From my view, there are many opportunities to enter careers that will provide students with high paying jobs. The goal should be to recognize that, for some, apprenticeships could be the 21st century conveyor belt to ride into America's middle class.

Chapter 7

The Achievement Ethic
& The American Dream

At age 70, by chance I met a clinician who has spent her career dealing with learning disabled children. We spoke and corresponded a few times, and she sent me an article distributed by the institute where she practices. The article lists some of the attributes detected by experts who observed dyslexia. One example given was from a professor who teaches astrophysics at the Harvard- Smithsonian Center for Astrophysics. There were so many dyslexics in the field that it prompted research by the Harvard-Smithsonian Center. The study found that dyslexics are better at memorizing enormous quantities of visual data, and accurately finding anomalies in space such as black holes. It noted that people with dyslexia see the world more holistically. They miss the trees but see the forest. Matthew H. Schneps of Harvard University stated, "It's as if people with dyslexia tend to use a wide-angle lens to take in the world, while others tend to use a telephoto; each is best at revealing different kinds of details."[16]

A similar finding was made by a world-renowned radiologist and pioneer in ultrasound imagery. Beryl Benacerraf noted that he lived in a world of patterns and images and saw things that no one else saw. "I can see patterns," he said.[17] The paper noted that many of America's greatest entrepreneurs had been identified as dyslexic: Thomas Edison and Henry Ford, earlier in the 20th century, as well as Steve Jobs and Charles Schwab in the present day were also considered dyslexic. Even Pablo Picasso suffered from learning disabilities. The paper quotes teachers who describe Picasso as "having difficulty differentiating the orientation of letters." He painted subjects as he saw them, sometimes out of order, backwards and upside down. His paintings demonstrated the power of his imagination, which is perhaps linked to his inability to see written words properly. While I am not Pablo Picasso or Steve Jobs, virtually every comment made in this paper applies to me. When I was subjected to tests by psychologists and a psychiatrist, I was asked to view figures involving spatial relationships, all of those problems I obviously solved during the examination. Those psychologists in the late 30's and 40's who tested me did not identify my reading difficulties as emanating from dyslexia. Since this disability is so common today, it is important that more effort be made to identify dyslexics in grade school and appropriate steps taken to identify and deal with it early on.

THE AMERICAN DREAM

It is my hope that this book will be a useful resource for parents with children that exhibit learning problems while still in the lower grades. Parents are the front line. They must be vigilant and proactive because schools in their districts or states may not be attentive to learning disabilities. Parents want their children to succeed. I have met scores of such parents, the majority of whom are relieved when they hear that someone as mixed up and written off as I was can end up being successful. I have seen the hope expressed in their faces almost saying, "If this man could be successful, so can my child." In some cases mothers of learning-disabled children were brought to tears as they experienced the feeling of hope that their child would be okay. I still communicate with some of those parents and have included stories about them in this book.

But parents can only do so much. It falls upon teachers of these students to take corrective action. Unfortunately, teachers are limited by their own knowledge of the learning disabled and the extent to which the school system or the state recognizes the problems of the learning disabled and is committed to addressing those problems. The message of this book to teachers and school counselors is timely. As we have noted, the role of school counselors has shifted from dealing with students who exhibit behavior problems to preparing students for college. Today we recognize that the chief conveyor belt for delivering Americans into the middle class (i.e. industrial jobs) has been in decline for 60 years.

Now the nation is demanding that the industrial base be reconstituted. I have tried to point out options for school counselors to take advantage of this opportunity. Granted, some counselors have told me that it is hard to tell a parent that their child is not college material and should go into an apprenticeship. But I have told parents who have asked me that same question that the apprenticeship program gave me the discipline to get myself in order. After I was successful as an apprentice, I went on to college and graduate school. For some people, an apprenticeship program could be a moratorium, where they develop skills, build confidence, and move on from there.

I managed to be successful despite a major learning disability that has been an insurmountable obstacle for others struggling with that same affliction. I attribute my success in both the academic and business world to my fervent belief in America. Like Warren Buffett, I believe I won the lottery when I was born in the United States. My Italian-speaking parents, all of my relatives and neighbors came to America seeking freedom and opportunity. Uneducated as we were, we had the advantage of living in the greatest country on earth.

AMERICA: THE LAND OF OPPORTUNITY

We live in a country where millions and millions of people have gone from rags to riches. Look at the history of America. Everyone who worked hard may not have become a multimillionaire like a Rockefeller or Warren Buffet, but millions surely have made it into the middle class. Immigrants cross our borders, because they know America is the land of opportunity.

Unfortunately, today your children will face one problem that my parents and I did not encounter in grade or middle school. Today, America has its detractors. There are professors and some political figures who will tell you that American capitalism is an unjust economic system. There are hundreds of college professors in our prestigious universities who tell their students that the poor cannot make it in America. In fact, at present, there is a university system encouraging its professors not to say "America is the land of opportunity." This philosophy is aimed at undermining our market economy. Also, unlike in my day, students today are not given the opportunity to examine the different economic systems that exist globally. Grammar and middle school children are seldom told about the disasters that befell socialist and communist countries that were founded on economic principles different than those found in America. Many of the students that I counsel have not been taught the miracle of our market economy that has enabled poor people to become millionaires, and millions more to become part of America's middle class. As the former Director of the Peace Corps, I can testify that nowhere else in the world will you find such an extensive middle class or any of the opportunities so many young people today take for granted.

My immigrant grandmother often said, "We came to America because we knew the streets were lined with gold, but we also knew we had to bend down to pick it up." If you work hard, you will improve your life. Every parent in my community and in the surrounding neighborhoods, whether Polish, Greek, Lithuanian, Italian, Jewish taught their children the same thing. This was true in both the Catholic and public schools I attended. The goal was assimilation. The immigrants who came to America in the early 20th century worked hard at becoming Americans. They learned English and quickly assimilated into their newly adopted country. My father told us never to eat pasta in public to avoid being identified as Italian pasta eaters. The same was true when eating garlic. To this day, I have never developed a taste for garlic, even though most Americans are quite comfortable with it. My father was proud to become a citizen. I still have the papers he signed when he was naturalized in 1928. They are a treasured possession.

Unfortunately, many teachers in the lower grades, middle schools, and high schools have not been taught the mechanics or the blessings of a free market economy. Nor have they been steeped in the patriotism and the view of citizenship that we had in my neighborhood in either the public or parochial schools. Worse still, they have obtained college degrees from universities and colleges where faculties undermine the advantages of our economic system, our Constitution, and our civic culture. This subject goes beyond our discussion of learning disabilities and behavior problems, but it does deal with producing students who believe that everyone can achieve the American Dream.

Even when I was a failure academically and socially, I maintained the belief that I could make it if I tried. The major message in my community was, "In America everyone can make it if they try." The nuns and teachers who taught in our neighborhood schools constantly repeated the same message. It worked; the ethnic communities in the New Haven area produced doctors, lawyers, entrepreneurs, and successful businessmen, as well as craftsmen, all of whom became a large part of the middle and upper classes. Those who worked hard at failure usually succeeded. My point is that many contemporary school systems are not promoting a civic culture as they did a half century ago. Parents should place the promotion of a civic culture high on their agenda when selecting schools for their children. It will be important for their children's success.

After 83 years, I have had two opportunities in my lifetime where I witnessed an entire generation lift itself out of poverty and into the middle class. The first time was in the European ethnic community in which I lived. Decades later I witnessed it again with the influx of Vietnamese refugees. Following the fall of Vietnam, thousands of refugees found their way to America. Jose Sorzano, who I mentioned earlier in this book, was a Cuban refugee escaping the communist takeover of Cuba. The Sorzanos came to

America with just the clothes on their back, hence they were sympathetic to the Vietnamese refugees who arrived in America in the same condition.

The Sorzanos took into their home two Vietnamese families, the majority of whom did not speak English. They housed, clothed, and fed these people for almost two years. I saw the same pattern emerge with these Vietnamese families that I saw in my ethnic community in the 1940s. The children and the adults went from speaking a language that has no similarity to English to quickly learning our language. The parents worked as an extended family, working two and three jobs. They saved their money, they bought their own homes, they sent their children to public school. Then came the miracle, the children became the best students in the class. I watched other Asian students become top scholars in every academic setting. They hold degrees in engineering, economics, math, chemistry, and medicine. Today Asians dominate the universities they attend as top scholars and recipients of scholarship awards. Go to any university in America and ask to see a list of the top scholars; you will find Asians among them.

The message is clear. America is a country that encourages and supports achievement. If you do not take advantage of the opportunity that America offers, there are millions of others who will give anything for that opportunity.

This is a country where everyone is still free to pursue the American dream. At the same time, it is important to understand the meaning underlying the American dream. Perhaps one of the best comments on the subject of the American dream and the dignity of work was made by the CEO of the Wisconsin-based Snap-On Tool company, Nick Pinchuk. Pinchuk rejects the contemporary elite's denigrating description of working people—Joe Six Pack, Joe Greasy Paw, rednecks, etc. He said, "In some ways saying not-so-complimentary things about working men and women in America is the last politically correct form of bigotry." He went on to note that progressive elites believe that everyone needs a four-year degree to find the American dream. He noted that people have written books arguing that the American dream is slipping away. That is because, he states, they have redefined the American dream as becoming the CEO of a major company, or an attorney, or even a TV anchor. What the American dream has always been about is "keeping your family warm, safe, and dry, and having pride and dignity in your work."[18]

He is absolutely right. You do not have to be a multimillionaire or have a college degree behind your name to make it in America. There are craftsmen who were once apprentices and now own their own businesses and are doing as well or better than some of the graduates of the best universities in America. That's America at its best.

Epilogue

In Praise of My Teachers

I was lucky. I grew up in what really was a different world. As a six-year-old child, I was in elementary school during World War II. I participated in the air raid drills where we were marched into the basement to await the all-clear bells to return to our classrooms. Patriotism was displayed by the Catholic nuns and the grossly underpaid teachers who daily entered into my Italian neighborhood to teach in our public school. It may sound corny today but reciting the Pledge of Allegiance and singing the Star-Spangled Banner, accompanied by Miss Chrisman, who daily led the class playing a woefully out of tune piano, gave me a subconscious sense of patriotism that is still with me today.

As children, we were taught that we lived in a democracy that was established by a constitution that guaranteed our freedom. The air raid drills, we were told, were to protect us from bombs that could be dropped either by the Germans or Japanese who wanted to take away our freedom. On weekends my mother would take me to the movies where the Movie Tone News showed clips of bombing raids in European countries where children like me were killed. As an eight-year-old child, I watched these news clips. Moreover, I knew that all of my uncles were in uniform and fighting in Europe and the South Pacific. I remember the Blue Stars in the windows of neighbors whose children were in uniform and in harm's way. I remember the Gold Star in the window of Mrs. Carrano, whose son was killed in Germany. When the war ended, there were bonfires on my street to celebrate the victory. Neighbors cheered and danced around the giant blaze. Mrs. Carrano was not in the street celebrating the end of World War II. In fact, she was never seen in public throughout the remainder of her life. All this was real. During my grade school years, all of my teachers praised our country, its Founding Fathers, and the Constitution they wrote.

In addition to the patriotism that was promoted in the public schools, the capstone for me was the visit to our city by The Freedom Train that toured the country from 1947 to 1949. The red, white, and blue train carried, behind glass plate, an exhibit of 133 historical documents and memorabilia including the Bill of Rights, the Constitution, Lincoln's Gettysburg Address, the United Nations Charter and the Iwo Jima flag. When I was 12 years old, my grammar school class toured the train and viewed the near 200-year-old history of our country.

I also remember that my teachers focused on the responsibilities of citizenship. At the grammar school level, America's Founding Fathers were presented as honorable men who risked their lives and fortunes to provide the freedoms we now enjoy. In short, the school curriculum reinforced the patriotism that abounded during the war years. I do not see this same enthusiasm taught in the school systems today.

During those years, our entire population was pulling in the same direction. We believed that it was our country's free enterprise system and market economy that made America great. We knew it made us the wealthiest nation on earth. During the Cold War that followed the end of World War II, ethnic minorities with relatives enslaved in communist countries heard about their inability to get food, and basic necessities for their families. In America, our market economy guaranteed that there would be no shortages. Teachers in private and public schools alike imparted their patriotism and love for our country and its free market system onto their students.

I mentioned in an earlier chapter of this book that I learned English by listening to the nightly radio programs aired for young children. But I learned more than English. All of those programs conveyed both a moral perspective and a patriotic message. Jack Armstrong was the "All American Boy." Superman fought for "Truth, Justice and the American Way." Even the Lone Ranger represented good over evil. In many ways the radio programs I listened to provide a similar backdrop. I wonder what our young people are listening to today.

The teachers in my inner-city school dedicated themselves to giving their students a basic education. It was obvious that very few of their students would ever attend college. At the same time, teachers did their best to introduce us to the classics in art, music and history, along with math and science.

Looking back on the road I traveled, I have great sympathy for those teachers who today must deal with students like me. I openly disrupted the class by talking with other students, by throwing paper airplanes across the room, by throwing blackboard erasers out open windows, or by using a slingshot to punch holes in window shades. I thought about a radio program I recently heard or drew pictures of WW II airplanes and warships. Then there were times when I appeared totally detached from the classrooms. Teachers justifiably concluded that this poor child was physically in the room but mentally absent. What they did not know was I was listening to everything they said and enjoyed their lectures.

If I succeeded today it is because I had the advantage of wanting to succeed and dedicating my life to the pursuit of excellence. I also had another advantage I seldom speak about. All those years that I played on the waterfront and roamed through active rail yards with trains moving in front and behind me, I was not alone. When I sat on a sloping roof of an abandoned waterfront building with my feet dangling above the water seventy feet below, I was not alone. When I passed up a ride with other "Crazy Mikeys" who totaled their car killing the driver and another occupant, I was not alone. When I played in a cement window well in a deserted warehouse one freezing cold winter and could not climb out of its ice-coated walls, my mother, driven by a premonition, searched, found and pulled me to safety, preventing me from freezing to death.

On all these occasions, I was not alone. I was not alone when I went to the home of an automobile dealer to collect a debt of $20 owed to a young man who waxed his cars for two days. I was dressed in a gangster-style suit and carried a loaded 45 automatic in a shoulder holster. When his frightened wife answered the door on that Sunday morning, her husband followed with shaving cream lathered on his face, eager to pay me the money. He could have blown me off the porch with a 12-gauge shotgun that everybody had in their home and claimed self-defense for what he did. I was not alone when I refused to drive my car to help some friends empty a warehouse who were later caught and jailed. When I was six years old, the nuns told me that there was a guardian angel protecting me. I did not believe them then, but I surely believe it now.

Over the years, I have reflected on the teachers I had in grammar and middle school. They desperately wanted to help me. Miss Horowitz, who threw me out of the room where she lectured on Greek history, would never believe how much she contributed to my motivation to study the classics as an undergrad and graduate student. Miss Crissman, who referred to me in class as a "rotter" and led us in the Pledge of Allegiance and the Star-Spangled Banner on that woefully out-of-tune piano, would never believe how much that contributed to my sense of patriotism. Miss DiRuccio, who couldn't believe that I did not like team sports, would not believe that I have become a team player today. I also fondly remember Mr. Naples, who let me stay in his office instead of being thrown out of school, along with Mr. Gannett, who kept me after hours for misbehaving in his class by having me try, unsuccessfully, to solve long-division problems.

All of these teachers would be delighted that I have been so successful in my life. Yes, and even Captain Russo, who said I gave Italians a bad name before throwing me out of the National Guard. He would never believe the number of three- and four-star generals and admirals whom I have advised over the years. All of these teachers invested in me. I am the sum total of their investment. God keep them all. They collectively gave me the faith in myself and belief in my country that I have today. God willing, one day in His universe I would love to meet and thank all of those extraordinary teachers who came into my Italian community and tell them that I would not be where I am today were it not for them.

Appendix 1

My story illustrates some of the classic symptoms of dyslexia--difficulty reading, transposing letters and numbers in reading and math, and acting out with disciplinary problems when facing tasks in which I knew I would fail. However, these are just a few of the behaviors that suggest someone might have dyslexia. The internet is a good place to begin learning about dyslexia. Good resources include the Mayo Clinic and the National Institutes of Health.

Dyslexia—Overview

Dyslexia is a learning disorder that affects how the brain processes language for reading, spelling, writing, and math. People with dyslexia have normal intelligence and usually have normal vision. Most children with dyslexia can succeed in school with emotional support and tutoring or an individualized education program.

Dyslexia tends to run in families, and while there's no cure for dyslexia, it's never too late to seek help. Signs that a person may be at risk include:

- Late talking
- Learning new words slowly
- Difficulty learning nursery rhymes or playing rhyming games
- Reversing sounds or substituting words that sound alike
- Problems sequencing, including omitting letters, numbers, words, etc.
- Reading well below the expected grade level
- Difficulty reading aloud
- Problems with comprehension

- Difficulty seeing or hearing similarities and differences in letters and words
- Inability to sound out an unfamiliar word
- Difficulty spelling
- Difficulty focusing on tasks
- Mispronouncing or problems retrieving words
- Difficulty summarizing
- Difficulty memorizing
- Difficulty doing math

Dyslexia can affect people in other ways:

- **Learning Problems.** Because reading is basic to most school subjects, a child with dyslexia is at a disadvantage and may have trouble keeping up with peers.
- **Social problems.** Dyslexia may lead to low self-esteem, behavior problems, anxiety, aggression, and withdrawal from family and friends.
- **Problems as adults.** Difficulties with language and comprehension may prevent a child from reaching his or her adult potential. Extensive educational, social and economic consequences may result.

Dyslexia -- Websites

The following organizations have websites that contain a wealth of information that can aid parents, teachers and counselors:

The Mayo Clinic
https://www.mayoclinic.org/diseases-conditions/dyslexia/symptoms-causes/syc-20353552

The National Institutes of Health
https://www.ninds.nih.gov/Disorders/All-Disorders/Dyslexia-Information-Page

Appendix 2

Dyslexia—Helpful Organizations

Having identified the symptoms of dyslexia in Appendix 1, it is valuable for parents to know where they can get information beyond what we have uncovered so far. The following are websites and organizations parents might turn to for help.

(1) **Council for Exceptional Children**
(https://www.cec.sped.org/About-Us/Mission)
The Council is a professional association of educators dedicated to advancing the success of exceptional children. They accomplish their mission through advocacy, standards, and professional development. It was first organized in 1922 as The International Council for the Education of Exceptional Children.

(2) **Decoding Dyslexia**
(http://www.decodingdyslexia.net/home.html)
Decoding Dyslexia is a network of parent-led grassroots movements across the country concerned with the limited access to educational interventions for dyslexia within the public education system. It aims to raise dyslexia awareness, empower families to support their children and inform policy-makers on best practices to identify, remediate and support students with dyslexia.

(3) **International Dyslexia Association**,
Baltimore, MD (www.dyslexiaida.org)
IDA is a nonprofit organization with a focus on providing help with education and advocacy. It advertises 42 state branches and 22 global partners. The advocacy component is vital. Every parent should be well versed and have input in the writing

and assessments of their child's individual education plan (IEP). Appears to be a comprehensive website.

(4) **Dyslegia: A Legislative Information Site**
(www.dyslegia.com)
This website was created as a tool for tracking the progress of legislation related to dyslexia throughout the United States. It invites feedback on pending legislation, both federal and state.

To date, in the USA, 27 states have enacted laws that address the special learning needs of dyslexic children. These include: Alabama, Arizona, Arkansas, California, Colorado, Connecticut, Delaware, Florida, Illinois, Indiana, Iowa, Louisiana, Maine, Maryland, Nevada, New Jersey, New Mexico, Ohio, Oklahoma, Oregon, Pennsylvania, Tennessee, Texas, Utah, Washington, West Virginia, Wyoming. Parents should contact state representatives to understand what those laws require and how they would be helpful for their children.

(5) **Yale Center for Dyslexia and Creativity**
(www.dyslexia.yale.edu)
The mission of YCDC is to increase awareness of dyslexia and its true nature; specifically to illuminate the creative and intellectual strengths of those with dyslexia, to disseminate the latest scientific research and practical resources, and to transform the treatment of all dyslexic children and adults.

YCDC is the preeminent source of cutting-edge research, informed advocacy and trustworthy resources to help those with dyslexia reach their full potential. The Center's tools and resources are used widely by parents, educators and those with dyslexia to advocate for greater recognition and support for dyslexic children and adults. YCDC builds awareness in all communities and mobilizes grassroots efforts to close the reading achievement gap for all students, including low-income students of color, through policies that help dyslexic children succeed. The

Center also showcases the remarkable success stories of adults with dyslexia, including writers, scientists, celebrities, and government and business leaders.

YCDC was founded in 2006 by Drs. Sally and Bennett Shaywitz, world-renowned physician-scientists and leaders in the field of dyslexia research and diagnosis. Dr. Sally Shaywitz is the author of *Overcoming Dyslexia,* the seminal book on understanding and supporting those with dyslexia.

The website offers the Shaywitz DyslexiaScreen and describes it as "an efficient, reliable, and user-friendly universal screening measure for K-3 students who may be at risk for dyslexia. Dr. Sally Shaywitz created this unique evidence-based screening tool. It emphasizes phonological, linguistic, and academic performance based on classroom teacher observations, all in just a few minutes per student--unlike other measures which take up precious instructional time."

(6) **An Accessible Online Library for people with print disabilities** (www.bookshare.org)
Bookshare makes reading easier. People with dyslexia, cerebral palsy, and other reading barriers can customize their experience to suit their learning style and find virtually any book they need for school, work, or the joy of reading.

Appendix 3

The Orton-Gillingham Approach

The Orton-Gillingham Approach to reading instruction is named for the two people who brought their research together in the 1930s.

Samuel Torre Orton (1879-1948), a neuropychiatrist and pathologist at Columbia University, joined neuroscientific information with principles of remediation. As early as the 1920s, he studied children with the kind of language difficulties now commonly associated with dyslexia and formulated a set of teaching principles and practices to help them.

Anna Gillingham (1878-1963) was an educator and psychologist at Teachers College, Columbia University. Working with Dr. Orton, she trained teachers and compiled and published instructional materials. Gillingham merged Orton's teaching methods with her analysis of the structure of the English/American language. Along with Bessie Stillman, she wrote *Remedial Training for Children with Specific Disability in Reading, Spelling and Penmanship*. Published in 1935, the manual is updated and republished regularly.

Websites that provide more detailed information about the Orton-Gillingham approach are as follows:
https://www.understood.org/en/school-learning/partnering-with-childs-school/instructional-strategies/orton-gillingham-what-you-need-to-know

https://www.orton-gillingham.com

https://www.ortonacademy.org

Features of the Approach

Although the approach is structured according to how we use sight, sound, and touch to learn language, it is flexible to accommodate the needs of the individual student. Its primary feature is to utilize the three senses (sight, sound, touch) to teach the basic sounds of letters, then work sequentially to combine sounds to words, words to meanings.

1. At first, using the three senses, language skills are taught by having the student listen, speak, read and write. For example, a dyslexic student is taught to see the letter A, say its name and sound and write it in the air -- all at the same time. The method is thought to enhance the student's memory and ability to recall what is learned.

2. Once students learn sounds in isolation, they progress to blending the sounds into words, using syllables, roots, and prefixes. In this way, they learn the parts of language in an orderly fashion. As they learn new material, they continue to review old material so it becomes automatic. If there is confusion of a previously taught rule, it is retaught from the beginning so it can be recalled successfully with understanding. Vocabulary, sentence structure, composition, and reading comprehension are learned in a similar structured, sequential, and cumulative way.

3. Students also learn about the history of the English language and study its many generalizations and rules. Crucial to the teaching, they learn how they learn best so they can apply their knowledge and success with reading and writing to other subjects.

   John Gabrieli, Ph.D., from the Department of Brain and Cognitive Sciences at the

Massachusetts Institute of Technology said, "If we can identify children at risk effectively very early, we know the literature supports that early interventions are most effective not only for learning to read, but we also hope in any discouragement the child might have about his or her first major educational experience. If you could identify a problem before it plays out you can support a child in a way that doesn't make them feel defeated."

AOGPE Accredited Schools
The following is a state-by-state list of AOGPE accredited schools:

Alabama
Greengate School in Huntsville
www.greengateschool.org
256.799.6100
Grades k-middle school

Georgia
Schenck School in Atlanta
www.schenck.org
404.252.2591
Grades k-6
summer program offered

Hawaii
Assets School in Honolulu
www.assets-school.org
808.423.1356
Grades k-12

Massachusetts
The Carroll School in Lincoln
www.carrollschool.org
781.259.8342
Grades 1-9/day school

The Landmark School in Prides Crossing
www.landmarkschool.org
978.236.3010
Grades 2-12

Minnesota
The Reading Center in Rochester
www.thereadingcenter.org
507.288.5271
Grades pre-k – 11
Summer program and on-line offered

New York
The Kildonan School in Amenia
www.kildonan.org
845.373.8111
Grades 2-12

Stephen Gaynor School in NYC
www.stephengaynor.org
212.787.7070
Grades Pre-k – Middle School

The Windward School in White
Plains and Manhattan
www.thewindwardschool.org
914.949.6968
Grades 1-9

North Carolina
The Fletcher School in Charlotte
www.thefletcherschool.org
704.365.4658
Grades k-12

Ohio
Marburn Academy in New
Albany www.marburnacademy.org
614.433.0822
Grades 2-12

Rhode Island
The Hamilton School in Providence
www.wheelerschool.org
401.421.8100
Grades 1-8

South Carolina
Camperdown Academy in Greenville
www.camperdown.org
864.244.8899
Grades 1-8

Sandhills School in Columbia
www.sandhillsschool.org
803.695.1400
Grades 1-12

Trident Academy in Mt. Pleasant
www.tridentacademy.com
843.884.7046
Grades k-12

Vermont
The Stern Center in Williston
www.thesterncenter.org
802.878.2332
Grades pre-k-12
Evaluation and Private Tutoring

Virginia
Riverside School in Richmond
www.riversideschool.org
804.320.3465
Grades k-8
Summer Camp Grades k-6

Appendix 4

Books Pertaining to Dyslexia

Below is a list of useful books concerning dyslexia.

Betancourt, Jeanne. *My Name is Brain Brian.* **New York: Scholastic, Inc., 1993.**

Sixth-grader Brian starts school again misspelling his own name, acts out as the class clown. His teacher recognizes Brian's behaviors and arranges testing. He believes Brian is unusually intelligent and is not surprised the boy thrives with a combination of tutoring and mainstreaming.

Books, Phyllis, PhD. *Reversing Dyslexia: Improving Learning & Behavior without Drugs.* **Garden City Park: Square One Publishers, 2013.**

Most people do not realize that dyslexia is more than just a reading problem. It is often accompanied by social, psychological, and even physical issues that can make many everyday tasks seem unmanageable.

Davis, Ronald. *The Gift of Dyslexia: Why Some of the Smartest People Can't Read.* **New York: Penguin Group, 2010.**

This book outlines a unique and revolutionary program with a phenomenally high success rate in helping dyslexics learn to read and to overcome other difficulties associated with it.

Eide, Brock L. M.D. and Fernette F. Eide, M.D. *The Dyslexic Advantage: Unlocking the Hidden Potential of the Dyslexic Brain.* New York: Penguin Group, 2011.

With real science as their foundation, the authors believe that dyslexics have unique brain structure. While the differences make reading and literacy difficult, they suggest dyslexics have special talents. Their acronym MIND organizes the areas of reasoning according to their strengths, i.e., M=mechanical strengths; I=interconnected talents seen in artists and inventors; N=narrative gifts important to novelists and lawyers; D=dynamic perspectives seen in scientists and business pioneers.

Hunt, Lynda M. *Fish in a Tree.* New York: Penguin Random House, 2017.

Ally is embarrassed by her inability to read so devises distractions so no one will know. Her new teacher sees the creative girl behind the troublemaker. With his help, Ally learns not to be so hard on herself and that dyslexia is nothing to be ashamed of. As her confidence grows, Ally feels free to be herself and the world starts opening up with possibilities. Ally learns that great minds don't always think alike and she is not dumb. "If you judge a fish by its ability to climb a tree, it will go through life believing it's stupid."

Shaywitz, Sally M.D. *Overcoming Dyslexia: A New and Complete Science-Based Program for Reading Problems at Any Level.* New York: Random House, 2003.

A great book that explains what dyslexia is and gives parents tools for helping their children become fluent readers. One of the most helpful and informative books that parents can read early in their journey that really opens their eyes and points them in the right direction to seek the help their kids need.

Treland, Joan Lash. *Gifted Dyslexics.* **New York: Page Publishing, 2018.**

As a researcher of learning disabilities, Treland profiles well-known people who had remarkable talents but struggled with reading and learning: Thomas Edison, Winston Churchill, Eleanor Roosevelt, Katherine Mansfield, among others. She proposes that educators shift their focus from what a child cannot do, and instead focus on their strengths and capabilities.

Endnotes

1 Throughout this book I will be referring to the term dyslexia. Dyslexia is a learning disorder that is caused by the brain not properly processing written words or numbers so that it makes sense to the dyslexic person viewing letters or numbers. There are other manifestations that appear in dyslexic persons. In Appendix 1 we discuss all of these manifestations in great detail. At this point, it would be well for the reader to understand that dyslexia is a learning disability that is fairly common. In my case, my antisocial behavior was an unconscious effort to mask my learning disabilities.

2 William Delaney, "Garbage Man to PhD," *Evening Star*, June 9, 1971, A1

3 In the Italian community the Don met the needs of neighborhood residents and was an enforcer who kept the peace.

4 Delaney, op. cit.

5 Emily Hanford, "Hard to Read: How America's Schools Fail Kids with Dyslexia,"
America's Public Media Reports (APM Reports), September 11, 2017.
https://www.apmreports.org/story/2017/09/11/hard-to-read

6 Sally Shaywitz, MD, *Overcoming Dyslexia: A New and Complete Science-Based Program for Reading Problems at Any Level* (New York: Alfred A. Knopf; 2003)

7 Hanford, op. cit.

8 "This Week with Christiane Amanpour," ABC, May 29, 2011.

9 Zack Friedman, "Student Loan Debt Statistics in 2019: A $1.5 Trillion Crisis," Forbes, February 25, 2019.
https://www.forbes.com/sites/zackfriedman/2019/02/2 5/student-loan-debt-statistics-2019/#7310389e133f

[10] Mike Rowe (President and CEO of Mike Rowe Works Foundation, former host of "Dirty Jobs"), Varney & Co., Fox Business Network, March 28, 2017. https://video.foxbusiness.com/v/5376095785001/#sp=s how-clips

[11] Katy O'Grady, "Youth Apprenticeship: Path to Modern Success," *School Counselor*, Volume 54, Number 2, November/December 2016, page 20.

[12] Mike Petters (President and CEO, Huntington Ingalls Industries), "What the Next President Should Do About U.S. Manufacturing: An Agenda for the First 100 Days," Washington, DC: U.S. Manufacturing and Public Policy Conference sponsored by Indiana University School of Public Affairs, September 14, 2016.

[13] In 2016 Huntington Ingalls CEO Mike Petters announced he would annually give all but $1 of his base salary ("in the ballpark of $950,000") to an educational fund that includes scholarships for children of employees. Laura Pultre, "Why This CEO is Donating His Salary to Workforce Education," *Industry Week*, March 28, 2016. https://www.industryweek.com/ceo-donating-his-salary

[14] Anita Sands and Madeline Goodman, "Too Big to Fail: Millennials on the Margins," The ETS Center for Research on Human Capital and Education, April, 2018 https://www.ets.org/research/report/opportunity-too-big-to-fail

[15] Norman Augustine, "Race to the Bottom," *Aviation Week and Space Technology*, August 24, 2009.

[16] Matthew H Schneps, PhD, Director of the Harvard-Smithsonian, Center for Astrophysics, "Nine Strengths of Dyslexia," on the Nessy Learning, LLC website: https://www.nessy.com/us/parents/dyslexia-information/9-strengths-dyslexia

[17] Beryl Benacerraf, M.D., "Nine Strengths of Dyslexia," on the Nessy Learning, LLC website: www.nessy.com https://www.nessy.com/us/parents/dyslexia-information/9-strengths-dyslexia

[18] Nick Pinchuk (CEO, Snap-On Tools), Fox and Friends Program, Fox News Channel, April 19, 2017. https://video.foxnews.com/v/5403168581001/?playlist_id=86912#sp=show-clips

Index